My
SPIRITUAL JOURNEY

Printed in the United States of America.

ISBN: 978-1-63385-134-4

Library of Congress Control Number: 2016904598

Designed and published by

Word Association Publishers
205 Fifth Avenue
Tarentum, Pennsylvania 15084

www.wordassociation.com
1.800.827.7903

My
SPIRITUAL JOURNEY
A LIFE OF SERVICE, A LIFE OF CHOICE

RABBI RALPH P. KINGSLEY

WORD ASSOCIATION PUBLISHERS
www.wordassociation.com
1.800.827.7903

ACKNOWLEDGEMENT

We are who we are because of the myriad influences upon us. My spiritual journey would not have been possible but for the many people who helped shape my thinking and who otherwise helped me along the way. I have alluded to many of them in the pages that follow. But some deserve extra mention. I repeat their names here.

Foremost among them are my parents, Albert and Erna Kingsley of blessed memory, who brought me to life and courageously uprooted theirs to bring me to this blessed land where my journey began in earnest at the age of four. It was only much later that I realized how young they themselves were at the time as they too began on a journey of their own. To them I owe the sense of right and wrong and the desire to do something useful and meaningful with my life which propelled me to become a rabbi.

It is a Jewish tradition to thank one's teachers by inserting special words into the mourner's prayer, the Kaddish, to be recited after a period of study. (Some believe that to have been the origin of the Kaddish). I have described how each of them, especially Dr. Harry M. Orlinsky, Dr. Samuel Atlas, Dr. John Tepfer and Dr. Henry Slonimsky, all of blessed memory, influenced me at various stages of my Jewish, intellectual development. But one name appears more than any other. That is because it was Rabbi Herbert Baumgard who motivated me to embark on my spiritual path and who was present at the critical times of my journey. He inspired me to become a rabbi, was my mentor, the officiant at my wedding and the one who facilitated my coming to Temple Sinai in North Miami Beach where I spent most of my rabbinic life. As of the writing of these words, he is ninety years old and of sound mind. May he be granted many years of life.

A name not mentioned in this book is that of Dr. Ernst Shlochauer, my first Professor of English at Queens College and my faculty advisor during that formative period of my life. He was, like me, a German refugee. In addition to being a Shakespearean scholar, he loved Jewish life and provided a very important translation from German to English of the writings of one of the great, early German Reform rabbis, Abraham Geiger. Dr. Schlochauer not only taught me how to write but gave me encouragement at a critical time in my life. He died a very young man of a heart disease that would have been treatable had he been born a few years later. To this day, I remember him with great affection.

With far greater affection, indeed, with a deep and abiding love do I acknowledge my wife of fifty six years, my "beautiful, beloved Brenda" as I dubbed her soon after we were married. She has been a constant presence at my side for all of those years keeping me centered when I veered off course, and sharing my rabbinic life- its moments of challenge and its times of great joy- in every way, even as she set the agenda for the many good things we have enjoyed together in our private life. Best of all, she bore and, with occasional help from me, reared two wonderful sons, Evan and Jonathan. They, with their wives, Dara and Wendy, have given us four loving grandchildren- Ava, Julia, Elizabeth and Max. It is for them that these words have been set forth with the hope that they too will learn to love the Jewish tradition as I have.

Finally, I cannot conclude without expressing my profound thanks to Merle Saferstein, a congregant of many years and herself a published author, who volunteered to read and edit an early version of my manuscript. Any mistakes in style, grammar or spelling are due to no fault of hers; they are mine.

TABLE OF CONTENTS

CHILDHOOD MEMORIES

When the biblical Abraham heard the call to *go forth* from the land of his birth and his father's home, it was to an unknown place that God would show him. His father Terach, wife Sarah and his cousin Lot accompanied him on that journey along with others about whom we read in the twelfth chapter of GENESIS. That journey, begun as an act of faith, would lead to the beginnings of a new way of life that we have come to know as Judaism. Though three thousand years have passed, I am a beneficiary of that ancient journey, as are my wife, my two sons and now, my four grandchildren. So, for that matter, are the fourteen million Jews who people the earth today though few of them, I would venture to say, think in those terms. I do because I am a rabbi and being Jewish is not only the centerpiece of my life. It is something that I feel proud of claiming as my own. I find it both enriching and pleasure giving. It makes me feel very special.

But it was not always so. While I was born to two Jewish parents, our home was not particularly Jewish in a ritualistic way. My mother, Erna, nee Maier, did not light candles on Friday night nor was my father, Albert Kissinger, an outwardly observant Jew. The fact is that by the time I was of an age where I was conscious of such things, my parents were too busy establishing themselves and providing for me in our new home. We rented a first floor apartment at 601 West 149 Street in New York City atop a hill that went down from Broadway to Riverside Drive. It was not easy for us in 1938 and in the years that followed. Both my parents had to work in order to make ends meet. My father found employment at Eagle Pencil Company where he earned $13 or $14 dollars a week with his degree in mechanical engineering. My mother toiled as a charwoman, cleaning homes, often on her hands and knees.

But in truth, our lives were not very different from those of other new immigrants and we were grateful for having been welcomed into the United States.

I still remember the night of our arrival on Jan. 6, 1938 after more than a week of sailing on the SS Washington. It was after dark and drizzly when we got off the ship. The sight of the light rain against the neon lights of the stores we passed remains with me to this day. We were met by my mother's younger brother (by eleven years), my Uncle Ted who had come to these shores several years before us and was thus already familiar with American ways. He escorted us to a one room apartment on 96 Street where we spent the first several days in our new environment; just long enough to find a more permanent place to live. He was our closest relative although it was an uncle of my mother's, living in Philadelphia, who had signed the necessary papers guaranteeing that we would not become a burden to our new land. He was the guarantor without whom we would not have been given a visa.

I am sure my parents had not so envisioned the course of their lives. Theirs had been a life of comparative middle class comfort in Nuremberg, Germany where I was born on Nov. 28, 1933, the same year that Hitler, may his name be cursed, took power. I have few memories from those days except that we lived across the street from a park. I recall looking out of the window and seeing the trees covered with a white powder-- my first awareness of snow. I recall as well, looking forward to my father's coming home from work and greeting him atop the hill that went down into an underground garage. He would let me ride with him to park the car. Most dramatically, I remember the bread crumbs on the window sill which were, I was told, food for the stork that was to bring me a brother or a sister. Alas, the stork seems to have gotten lost along the way for the longed for sibling never did arrive.

It was during those earliest of my childhood years that lives began to change for many of Germany's Jews. Interestingly, my father never spoke of the impact of the infamous Nuremberg Laws of 1935 which deprived the Jew of citizenship and political rights and increasingly made pariahs out of members of the Jewish community. But he did speak of how, as an engineer, he had occasion to visit underground factories where he saw the machinery of war being built. He had sensed that war in Europe was imminent and that, in all likelihood, it would not go well for Germans in general; even less for Jews. And so he, my mother and I, like Abraham our great ancestor, went forth from our ancestral home with all of its comforts to a place we did not know arriving in New York City on Jan. 6, 1938. My father was thirty five, my mother was thirty one. I was just four. It was only many years later that it dawned on me what an extraordinarily brave move this was by my parents, to journey across the ocean to an unknown place and literally to begin their lives anew. Had they not done so, chances are that I would not be writing this memoir for most of those who remained behind perished.

My life during my early growing-up years was unremarkable. Although we spoke German at home, I quickly learned English and was happy when my father and my Uncle Rudy, at the suggestion of my first cousin Werner, changed our family name to Kingsley. Werner had come to the United States from England where he had gone via the Kindertransport and thought a name change to be appropriate. Our lives were, after all, beginning anew in a land that was, for us, also new. Moreover, in the early 40s, German sounding names like Kissinger were not desirable. Today, I am sorry about that turn of events less because our distant cousin Henry brought fame to the name Kissinger (sometimes in a not-so-positive way) but, more importantly, because I feel my children and grandchildren may lose a historical connection to a family whose roots we now trace to the eighteenth century. On the other hand, our forebears Abraham and Sarah both underwent name changes from Avram and Sarai, so perhaps I should not quibble. In any case, it is too late for me to change back even though, ironically, the daughter of Werner (who became Norman), Gabrielle Kingsley, did reclaim the Kissinger name before she married.

I went to a neighborhood Public School when the time came and played stick ball, stoop ball and curb ball, our games of choice. There were no ball fields in the neighborhood. The best we could do is play in the street and hope no cars came to interrupt our games. But there was a synagogue right across from where we lived which provided a wonderful wall against which my friends and I played, even during Jewish holidays, much to the dismay of the worshippers who would chase us away with regularity. But in those days, I knew no better.

I did not get to see the inside of that imposing place of worship which still stands but is today a Black Church until my maternal grandparents, Henry and Toni Weber Maier, arrived from Stuttgart in late 1940 or early 1941- at the last moment of opportunity for the Jews of Germany. My grandfather would bring me with him into the *schul* where I would sit at his side, and he would drape me in his *talit*. I often think of the warmth of that experience, snuggling next to the only grandfather I ever really knew, albeit only for a few years. He died of complications from diabetes in 1944. My paternal grandfather Isadore had died when I was but two years old. My maternal grandmother Else died at the hands of the Nazis in Izbica so I barely knew her either. My grandmother Toni, on the other hand lived into her eighties, long enough to see the birth of our firstborn son, her great grandchild. She died a few months thereafter, and I officiated at her funeral in the fall of 1962.

In that synagogue across from where we lived, I have what is probably my other earliest Jewish memory: of attending services with my grandfather on *Sukkot* and tasting the sweetness of wine in the *Sukkah* so beautifully decorated with branches and fruits. To this day, the tastes and smells of *Sukkot* remind me of that experience and of the story the rabbi told to the children at that time. It was of the Jew who, when challenged during a Medieval Disputation, bested a priest in a debate by asking him to translate the Hebrew phrase *Eineni Yodea*. When the priest correctly translated the phrase as meaning *I don't know*, it seemed as if he did not know the answer to the question: *What is the meaning of eineni yodea?* Answer: *I don't know.* And so, he was bested by the wiser rabbi who thus saved the Jewish community from collective punishment or, worse, forced conversion. For me, it was just a clever story. I was later to learn that such disputations were commonplace in the Middle-Ages and, most frequently, did not end as happily as the one I heard that particular day.

Strange the memories which remain with me! The tropical climate in South Florida makes the decoration of the *Sukkah* with fruits impossible. They rot within a day as I found out when I built my first *Sukkah* in North Miami Beach where we were to settle many years later. We were driven, therefore, to use artificial fruit instead. As a result those delicious smells remain only as a distant memory from my years in New York both as a child and, many years later, as a young rabbi in Garden City, L.I. It was there I built my own *Sukkah* and proudly displayed my black and blue thumb from the pulpit as evidence of the fact that I had truly engaged in that *mitzvah*.

The amazing thing is that despite the lack of any outward expression of Jewishness in our home, I always knew I was Jewish and never considered being something else. How or why I cannot say. But somewhere deep within there must have been a Jewish gene that even in those early days would remind me who I was from time to time. Thus when my father asked me one day as he and I were walking together on Broadway in NYC: *What religion do you want to be when you grow up? You can be whatever you want,* I answered: *I want to be what you are. I want to be Jewish!* I had no doubt. Whether out of love for my father or for some inexplicable spiritual reason, that conviction turned into the organizing principle of my life and brought me much joy. It also caused me sorrow and one day taught me a tearful lesson about the situation of the Jew in the world, which hopefully has today changed. But in the 1940s, it became an important moment in my spiritual journey.

My father worked at one time for the Ward Baking Company as a plant engineer. In order to get that job, he had to hide the fact that he was Jewish, a common occurrence in those days before the birth of Israel. The consequences of that decision might not have been so obvious were it not for the fact that *Yom Kippur* occurred on a work day. My father decided he had to go the plant lest it be discovered he was a Jew and lose his job. I knew little of what it meant to be Jewish or how to observe Jewish rituals. But I did know, instinctively, that *Yom Kippur* was the most important day of the Jewish year. One fasted and one assuredly did not go to work or to school. Tearfully, I broached the subject to my father saying: *How can you go to work? It is Yom Kippur, the most sacred day of the Jewish year.* Equally tearfully, my father explained that if he did not appear at work, he might lose his job and his source of income. I understood and did not blame my father. But at the same time, I was deeply pained by the unfairness of it all vowing silently that when I grew up, it would be different. If anything, I became even more firm in who I was. I have never forgotten that day.

By 1944, when I was well on my way to my eleventh birthday, my parents finally enrolled me in Sunday school at the Hebrew Tabernacle on 161 St. and Ft. Washington Ave. The upper part of Manhattan, still known as Washington Heights today, was then lovingly referred to as *The Fourth Reich* because it became home to so many refugees from Hitler's Germany. We lived in an apartment building on 149ᵗʰ Street and Broadway surrounded by many of my parents' friends, all of whom had left Germany at about the same time as my parents. But the largest concentration of German Jews was in the 160's and higher. *Yekkes* they were called, a nickname, some argue, originating from the fact that the men were very formal, never appearing without a tie and jacket- *Jacke* in German. There were a number of synagogues in the area, each with its own ideological style, some more and some less traditional and frequently with a German speaking rabbi. My parents, coming from a liberal Jewish tradition, chose a Reform congregation with an American rabbi (actually, Aaron Opher had been born in Palestine). The membership, however, was largely German and Cantor Ehrenberg was schooled in the German musical tradition to which they were accustomed. And so began my first formal Jewish learning experience. Happily, the Jewish parents of today enroll their children at a younger age, and that is much to the good.

That notwithstanding, I have fond recollections of those days, especially of the Bible stories that were central to the curriculum. I learned about the Patriarchs, Abraham, Isaac and Jacob, Joseph's coat of many colors and the nomadic life of the ancient Israelites. We were taught that Jewish men covered their heads as a result of the heat of the desert sun (true, but not why Jewish males cover their heads in prayer) and that camels were the animals of choice because they could survive on very little water. Strange, what left a lasting impression, but all of that was new information for me. That our ancestors, gave the world the notion of one God and an ethical system which derived from it was something I would only begin to appreciate at a much later time.

I don't remember learning much about the Jewish holidays, perhaps because there was little or no Jewish observance to speak of in our home. One thing stands out as an exception however. While details are vague (I was eleven or twelve at the time) I remember distinctly getting dressed up for a *Purim* celebration. We put on a play for an organization away from the synagogue and I dressed up in my mother's rubber boots that had high heels and came up to my knees. I don't have a clue as to who I was trying to be. It must have made an impression though because all through my rabbinate, I loved to get dressed up and have fun on *Purim*-albeit with more comfortable shoes.

I think it carried down to the next generations as well for during a trip to Israel with my son Evan and his family many years later my two granddaughters bought themselves outrageous *Purim* wigs and happily wore them as we strolled through the streets of Jerusalem along with costumed Israeli children. They even wore them to the *Megillah* reading in Jerusalem's main synagogue on *Purim* eve where we used Israeli *groggers* to drown out the name of Haman.

A less happy *Purim* memory is also associated with Israel. Our congregational trip in 1974 coincided with *Purim* but there was no joy that year. On the day before *Purim*, the *WHITE BOOK,* so called because of its color, was distributed. It contained the names of all those who fell during the tragic *Yom Kippur* War of the previous year. No Israeli household was spared. If they were fortunate enough not to have lost a family member, they knew a neighbor who had. Such is the reality of Israel.

My other recollection from those beginning days of my somewhat meager Jewish education is of participating in a Sabbath morning worship service. Our class read prayers in English (Hebrew was frequently not part of the curriculum in the Reform congregations of that time) from the old *Union Prayer Book* and I particularly remember being asked to read the beautiful prayer for peace: *Grant us peace, O Thou eternal Source of Peace*…Even if the reading was something of the rote variety, and even if I didn't completely understand the words, I was pleased to be able to stand in front of the congregation. I didn't know it then but my spiritual journey was taking a new turn.

LAURELTON: THE TEEN YEARS

In 1946, the journey continued in a new location. THOSE WHO were part of the refugee generation that had fled from Hitler were by now well on their way to establishing themselves in their new country of choice. Here, in the United States, they did not need to fear for their lives and, along with other Americans, they could enjoy the fruits of freedom and breathe in the air of democracy. They understood, as Max Lerner, columnist for the *New York Post* was to write in an important book called *America as a Civilization*, that the essence of America was the ability to have *access* to that which at another time and in another place one could only have dreamed of. Till this day, immigrant generations want to come here because no aspiration is beyond the realm of the possible. This is truly the land of opportunity.

My father, who was a kind and gentle man, much loved not only by me and my mother but by each of the many friends who comprised *The Crowd,* as my mother referred to them, had by now held several jobs. After his years in the Bronx plant that produced Wonder Bread, and where he had to hide his Jewish identity, my father came to the Jewish-owned, Brooklyn plant of Liebmann Breweries, manufacturers of Rheingold. Along with being one of the best selling beers in New York City at the time, Rheingold was famous for its advertising jingle which none of us who lived in New York during those days will forget.

My beer is Rheingold the dry beer, think of Rheingold whenever you buy beer,

It's not bitter not sweet, it's the dry flavored treat, won't you buy extra dry Rheingold Beer?

It was also well known for its annual MISS RHEINGOLD CONTEST, a beauty contest which led to the crowning of one of the pretty women whose photos were posted in subway cars and in newspapers over the course of many weeks each year.

While he held an important job as plant engineer, my father was never a big earner. We needed my mother's income to help us manage expenses. Having demonstrated her prowess as a cleaning woman in the office of Dr. Ernst and Edythe Springer on West 81st St. in NYC, she was invited to become his dental assistant, a position she held for many years. Since both of my parents had a way of attracting friends, their employers, as often happened in those days, also became their social friends. The relationship with the Springers was to last well into retirement. At a much later time, during my parent's retirement years in South Florida, they reconnected with the man who was my father's superior at Liebmann Breweries, Manny Weiss and his wife Sari who, as it happens, were members of my synagogue. Theirs became a very special friendship until death ended it. I mention it here because it says something of the kind of outgoing people my parents were.

My parents enjoyed socializing, although we always lived modestly, within our means. Except for an infrequent visit to a local Chinese Restaurant and an occasional movie, I do not remember our going out much. Sleep-away Camp was not an option though I did attend a local Day Camp in Inwood for several summers while we still lived in Manhattan. Even family vacations took us not to fancy resorts but to a small farm in Cairo, NY, the non-Jewish part of the Catskills, where it was cheaper. My children and grandchildren have been exposed to so much more than I was. I hope they realize how lucky they are and that they don't take all with which they are blessed for granted.

Still, I never felt deprived. Nor did I envy others who had more than we did. Perhaps I didn't know the difference. I only knew what I had, not what I didn't have. So when my parents began to think of moving out of

Manhattan to a place where the air was clean and where we could own a home of our own, I shared their excitement. I looked forward to the many weekend drives to New Jersey and Westchester County in search of a new home.

In particular, I recall a new area about to be developed called Armonk. I mention Armonk, because our granddaughters attended school there, our son Evan and his family having settled in an adjacent Westchester community called Pleasantville. Back then, in 1945, new homes in that muddy, undeveloped area forty five minutes from mid-town New York were selling for $12,000, which quickly became $18,000; too expensive for the Kingsley family. Today they are in the millions. And to think we could have lived there. Instead, we moved to a community in Queens called Laurelton, a thirty minute train ride from Manhattan or Brooklyn on the Long Island R.R. There we settled into a large, brick house on a wide tree-lined street divided by a grassy center strip.

The purchase was actually a joint venture. My parents bought the house together with their dearest friend from Nuremberg, Bruno Buchstein, and his mother whom I called Tante (Aunt) Hansi. Bruno was a strikingly handsome, prematurely gray-haired bachelor who had been divorced in Germany and never remarried. Instead, he lived with and cared for his long-widowed mother who was burdened with extreme hearing loss. She was like a second grandmother to me. When they came to the United States soon after we did, Bruno and Tante Hansi moved into an apartment in the same building in which we lived at 601 West 149 St. It was perfectly natural for Bruno and his mother and my parents to pool resources and to purchase a two family home. Together they could afford something much nicer than either could have managed alone.

For many weekends prior to our moving in, we would get into our car (I don't remember much about the cars we owned during those days except that they were never new) and drive to Laurelton. Gasoline was no longer rationed as it had been during World War II. Since we could not afford contractors to prepare the house for its new inhabitants, my parents and Bruno spent endless weekend hours stripping, plastering, painting and wallpapering walls to get the house ready for occupancy. I helped where I could but mostly watched. The best part was that we would go to a local deli for sandwiches which we ate for lunch and sometimes dinner. For me it was a special treat.

Then, one day, in May of 1946, the work was done. We packed and left our apartment on 149 St. and moved to the suburbs in search of a better life. I left my schoolmates at P.S. 52 in upper Manhattan (which I had attended illegally using the address of friends who lived in that neighborhood because the school I had been assigned to had a bad reputation, even then) and said goodbye to the Hebrew Tabernacle. In Laurelton there would be a new home, a new school (P.S. 156, Queens) and a new synagogue, Temple Israel of Jamaica.

While the house my parents had purchased with Bruno was meant to accommodate one family on each of the bottom two floors (there was also a third floor), the decision, in a novel twist, was to divide the house vertically instead. Two living rooms (one for each family), one bathroom, and one kitchen (used by the Buchsteins), were on the first floor; three bedrooms a second bath and kitchen (used by us) were on the second floor. The third floor was used by us for overflow. And so we were two distinct families living as one, and it worked just fine.

But four years later, early in 1950, Bruno went to sleep and did not wake up. He had just turned fifty on New Year's Day. It was my second encounter with death, the death of my maternal grandfather having occurred six years earlier. In the case of the latter, I remember coming home from school and finding my mother and grandmother looking very sad but in control as they told me of my grandfather's death and that we would have to forego any parties for a while. My grandfather had suffered from severe diabetes which led to the amputation of both legs and lengthy periods of hospitalization. I must assume his death was anticipated. Bruno's death, however, came without warning. I remember awakening to screams and sobbing. But I have no other memories of either death or of the funerals or *Shiva*. I cannot even say with certainty that there was a *Shiva*, either for Bruno or for my grandfather. In retrospect, I feel somewhat deprived. It was before I had displayed rabbinic aspirations so perhaps I was just not on that wavelength. Or, it may be that I was not included in the process, though at sixteen, I certainly was old enough when Bruno died.

In later years, during my active rabbinate, I always urged that children be involved in the funeral service to as great an extent as possible including going to the cemetery. Death is part of life's process. It is at one and the same time life's greatest mystery and its greatest reality. Each of us must face it at some point and therefore, the more early preparation we have, the less likely that later experiences will traumatize us.

While she never knew it, Tante Hansi contributed to my Jewish journey in a significant way. She did not attend synagogue with any regularity having come from a background which made no such demand on women. Synagogue was for the men. Yet she was very pious and would stand with prayer book in hand reciting her prayers privately with great regularity. Not being able to hear must have been difficult. Yet it was obvious that an inner voice did speak to her; and she to it. She was a brave woman who dealt with adversity heroically, never bemoaning her lot. When she died she was well over eighty; surely at peace with herself and her Maker.

When I came to Laurelton, I was twelve and a half. In the Junior High School that I attended in uptown Manhattan, P.S. 52, I was enrolled in a rapid advance class. That meant that I would have skipped the first half of the eighth grade and graduated from Junior High School a semester earlier. There were January graduations in those days. But when we came to Laurelton, I was more anxious to meet new friends who were my age and chose to slide back to the regular track. I finished the seventh grade and was promoted to 8A instead of 8B. Since P.S. 156 was an eight-grade school, I spent a full year there and graduated.

Of more immediate concern was the fact that I would be 13 during our first year in Laurelton, and that I would need to prepare for *Bar Mitzvah*. There was no Reform synagogue in Laurelton (Conservative was not an option in my non-observant home) but there was one in Jamaica, Queens, a twenty minute bus ride away. So my parents joined Temple Israel and enrolled me in Sunday school where I continued my Jewish education and from which my spiritual journey was to take a new turn.

Since there were several other families with children my age in the neighborhood we car pooled on most Sunday mornings: Steve Bernstein, who lived across the street and was to remain my good friend until he died tragically at age 71, as a result of a freak bicycle accident, Stanley Wyler, still my friend to this day, Franklin Ormsten and Roberta Diamond, both of whom passed out of my life, all would be picked up by one of our parents and, at morning's end, would be retrieved at the Temple and delivered home. While none of us behaved very well in class (I seem to remember some phone calls home from teachers) we looked forward to the social experience and never resisted going. We even acquired some Jewish knowledge, even if in small doses.

The curriculum was a continuation of what I had started to learn at the Hebrew Tabernacle--more Bible stories and holidays with an occasional assembly and arts and crafts projects. Hebrew was still not required. When it came time for my *Bar Mitzvah*, Rabbi Alexander Kline gave me the Torah blessings to learn in transliteration and a speech written by him (rumor had it that it was really written by his wife) which I memorized for delivery on that special morning--Nov. 30, 1946. I practiced with the rabbi once each week, beginning in October, getting myself to the synagogue by bus and by foot. I still remember the first words of my *Bar Mitzvah* speech: *Today on the Sabbath after my thirteenth birthday, I am to become a Bar Mitzvah.*

As was customary in the Reform congregations of that time, I did not wear a *kippah* or *talit;* nor did I read from the Torah or chant a *Haftarah* as is today's expectation on a *Bar/Bat Mitzvah* morning. The fact is I hardly knew anything about what went on at services on Sabbath morning or what part in the order of prayer the Tradition assigned to the *Bar Mitzvah.* Yet, whatever I did, I gather I did well, or at least so everyone told me. And, I must say, I enjoyed the experience although I had only the vaguest idea of what it meant, or was supposed to mean in the life of an emerging young Jew. Happily, the Reform Movement has advanced far beyond those minimalist days and requires much more of its students. But, keep in mind that was before we had begun to understand just what World War II had done to the Jewish Community in leading to the slaughter of six million Jews and the destruction of Europe's rich Jewish life. Just as significantly, it was before the establishment of Israel and the rebirth of Hebrew and Jewish learning with all that implies. It was a different time in a very different Jewish world.

Oh yes, there was, of course, a party. Family and friends went back to our house in Laurelton where all were treated to a lavish spread of cold cuts, cole slaw and potato salad, probably from the same deli where we had bought those delicious lunch sandwiches a year earlier. Except for a Schwinn bicycle (my first two wheeler) that was given me by my parents, I don't remember what gifts I got although I do recall receiving cash in the amount of $72. I handed that sum to my parents for safekeeping and never saw it again. Perhaps it went to my college tuition. Actually, it would have gotten me through Queens College where tuition in 1951 was $7 per semester.

The Temple Israel experience did not end at age thirteen. It was understood in those days that one returned to Sunday school after one became a *Bar Mitzvah* until year's end and then that one continued for at least another year, perhaps two, until Confirmation, a group ceremony held on or around the late spring festival of *Shavuot.* This was not negotiable. It was the norm.

So it was that the car pools and Jewish learning continued until June 13, 1948 when eight of us, on that *Shavuot* morning, took part in a ceremony marked by a good deal of pageantry before a congregation of members and friends. In keeping with the theme of *Shavuot*, we celebrated the ancient event that took place at Mt. Sinai over three thousand years ago when the Jewish People took the Torah to themselves with the words *naaseh v'nishma, we will do and we will hear* the commandments given us by God through Moses. We students, with our prayers and our speeches, which this time we did write by ourselves, guided by our new rabbi, Albert Silverman, thus *confirmed* the faith of our forebears.

In addition, each of us placed a flower in the Ark to represent the other aspect of the holiday which was also known as *Hag Ha Bikurim*, the festival of the first fruits. In ancient days, our ancestors would bring the first fruits of their harvest to the High Priest in the great Temple in Jerusalem as part of their festival observance. Now through the flowers, each of us presented, our *Bikurim,* the first fruits of our learning.

As I reflect back to that year I am amazed that I do not remember more for it was in May of 1948 that the new State of Israel was born. Perhaps it is because Reform Judaism was still in its non-Zionist phase or because my home was so minimally Jewish. Arguably the greatest event in the modern history of the Jewish People seems to have passed me by (or I it). Fortunately, that has changed. Today Israel plays a central role in my belief system and is at the very center of Jewish life. But more on that subject later.

I do remember my Confirmation ceremony as yet another positive experience on my Jewish Journey which was to leave its mark as the years went by. It marked the beginning of my emergence into young Jewish manhood both in a religious and a social sense. In typical teen age fashion, the four girls in our class complained that we boys were too young for them. Nevertheless, in addition to the time we spent together in Temple rehearsing and preparing, there were also the parties held in the finished basements that became so prevalent in the days following World War II, where we explored and developed social skills in a non-threatening environment. Though by now I have lost track of my classmates, for many years some of those relationships lasted. Now and again, someone from those days would turn up at my synagogue on a Sabbath Eve and we would share happy memories. Even today, I look back to those long-ago days with feelings of nostalgia.

It is unfortunate that *Bar Mitzvah*, which for a long time was a minor event in Reform congregations, has taken on such major proportions for all of the wrong reasons- mainly the garish party aspect- while Confirmation, which is one the most imaginative creations of the Reform Movement, has become much less prominent. It is after all precisely during those years of Jewish learning and camaraderie that follow after *Bar* and *Bat Mitzvah* when our young people should be confronting Jewish ideas and values. But sadly, at the very time that their minds are able to grapple with the more serious aspects of Jewish life which elude most pre-teens, we lose them. *Bar/Bat Mitzvah* after all requires mainly that they have a good memory and can sing.

This was not the case within Reform Congregations when I was growing up or even during the earlier part of my Rabbinate. To be sure, the Confirmation ceremony was only the carrot that enabled us to hold on to our young during the post *Bar/Bat Mitzvah* years. But it served us well. If it has lost its power, it behooves us to find something to replace it lest the last Jewish connection our young experience before college is their moment of triumph when they are thirteen.

A NEW AWAKENING

Temple Israel was to continue to play an important part in my spiritual journey, if not directly than in an enabling way. Like many teenagers in search of a social connection, I tried getting involved in its youth program. In those days, however, the youth group at Temple Israel seemed to attract an older crowd- sometimes even beyond high school. So instead, along with my friend Stanley, I began to go to Friday night square dances at The Ethical Culture Society in Brooklyn. I was by then attending Brooklyn Technical High School, harboring thoughts of becoming an engineer like my father, an idea which Tech helped to quickly dissuade me from pursuing. Even though it meant travelling to Brooklyn yet one more time, it was not a big deal. We were used to traveling throughout the five boroughs whether by Long Island Railroad, subway, bus or a combination of any or all of them. It was safe and efficient and, in any case, very few of us had access to cars.

Given the nature of Ethical Culture, it should not be surprising that we met lots of Jewish teenagers. Some were Jewishly connected; others came from largely secular backgrounds. All of them were very bright and lots of fun to be with. They became the core of my social life during my teenage high school years. One day, one of those fellow square dancers, Betty Jane Levine, the daughter of a Brooklyn dentist who belonged to one of the Brooklyn Reform synagogues, mentioned that she was going to a GNFTY conclave that coming Labor Day weekend. *What is GNFTY?* I asked. Further conversation revealed that GNYFTY stood for the Greater New York Federation of Temple Youth, part of NFTY, the national youth arm of the Reform Movement. A conclave was a weekend retreat held at an away camp facility with rabbis and other youth group members from the same general area. One engaged in Jewish study, attended worship services and, most important of all, socialized with Jewish teenagers from throughout the area which, for us, meant New York City. From the sound of things, it would be great fun.

Armed with that information and having heard that they provided scholarships, I went to my Temple Israel Sisterhood which was in charge of youth activities at the synagogue and asked if they would send me. To my great delight, they said yes. They asked, in return, that I share my experience with the Sisterhood at one of their subsequent meetings, a request I was glad to fulfill when the time came. Little did I know then that the experience at conclave would totally change my life.

Before explaining how, I need to fill in some other blanks. By then several years had passed since Bar Mitzvah and Confirmation and I was already graduating from high school and about to enter college. I had applied to and been accepted at Queens, one of the four City Colleges, CCNY, Hunter and Brooklyn being the other three. It was actually my only application and since my grades were superior, I was not required to take an entrance exam. Given the financial picture at home, going out of town to a private university was not an option so I never took anything like SAT exams. The fact is I did not even know what they were until my own children were ready for college many years later.

Many things came together in 1951. I commuted to Brooklyn Technical High School each morning on the Long Island Railroad to the Flatbush Ave. station in downtown Brooklyn. From there, after the thirty minute train ride, I walked another ten minutes to Ft. Greene Place and entered the huge building where I spent ten months each year from 1947-1951. While at Tech, one of three special High Schools which, along with Bronx High School of Science and Stuyvesant, required an entrance exam insuring that they were populated largely by Jews (today Asians have that honor,) I learned that I did not want to be an engineer and discovered radio broadcasting.

Tech was unusual in that it had its own radio station from which it would broadcast to the homebound as well as to New York City school rooms. While the people who managed the station (WNYE, FM) were of course professionals (some in fact were teachers at Brooklyn Tech) others were employed by the city expressly to run the station. We students had the opportunity to be radio actors or to help in the various aspects of production like sound effects, music and engineering. In fact students came from all over the five boroughs to be part of the highly regarded ALL CITY RADIO WORKSHOP, as it was called, but those of us at Tech had an inside track. I was both an actor on dramatic programs of an educational nature and a student in the on-the-air classes held to enable children who were homebound to keep up with their studies. While I never disliked going to my regular classes, you can imagine how important I felt when I would be excused in order to take part in an English or history class that took place not in a classroom but in the broadcast studio. Not only did it make those years pass quickly and pleasurably, but it gave me a love for acting which was to re-emerge when I got to college.

I spent several summers during that period at work at Liebmann Breweries where my father got me a job sorting sales slips and invoices together with others. In those days before computers, we would sit around a table manually putting C.O.D. slips into numerical order, first by thousands, then by hundreds and then by tens. It was tedious but helped the hot summer days pass quickly in the presence of other teens whose company I enjoyed. I was able to travel to and from work with my father each day and, best of all, I earned $35 per week over the course of eight weeks- no small amount in those days. That continued until 1951, the summer after I graduated from High School, when I found a job as a counselor at an Orthodox summer Day Camp in Long Island, HI-LI by name (Hebrew Institute of Long Island). It was my first exposure to Orthodox Judaism, a world with which I was completely unfamiliar.

Here I learned that heads always were to be covered either with caps or yarmulkes and that food needed to be Kosher, neither a practice in my home. I learned too about holidays of which I had never heard, in particular, *Tischa B'Av*, the day that commemorates the destruction of the Temple in Jerusalem on two occasions. It marks as well many other tragedies in Jewish history, all of which are said to have taken place on the ninth day of the Hebrew month of Av. On that day which corresponds to a time in late July or early August, unlike the more familiar great fast of *Yom Kippur*, smoking and working are permitted, while swimming and eating are not. Go figure! My fellow counselors were pleasant enough but they lived in a different world from the one I had grown up in and knew. Most of them went to traditional Day Schools and came from observant homes. I imagine my lack of Jewish knowledge must have stood out like a sore thumb. Yet perhaps that experience awakened another spark within my Jewish soul and helped prepare me for what was to happen on Labor Day weekend at the GNFTY Conclave that same year.

FROM CONCLAVE TO THE RABBINATE

What an experience that was! On the Friday before Labor Day, one hundred or so Jewish teenagers (I was one of the oldest) boarded a bus in front of the House of Living Judaism and embarked on an adventure that, for many of us, was to lead not only to life-long friendships but to a deepened awareness of who we were and for some of us, even more than that. The House of Living Judaism with the words from LEVITICUS 19, *Love Your Neighbor as Yourself* chiseled into its stone facade is still there on the corner of 65th St. and 5th Ave. even though it has been sold (it is now an upscale condominium). It had been, for many years, the headquarters of the Union of American Hebrew Congregations, now known as the Union for Reform Judaism. But by whatever name, it must never be forgotten that one of its most important programs was the creation of a youth arm, NFTY (National Federation of Temple Youth), then under the leadership of the amazing Rabbi Sam Cook. Before the days of Liberal Jewish day schools, and before the creation of a Reform Jewish camping movement, it was NFTY that vitalized Jewish life. It helped to inspire young Jewish leaders, many of whom became rabbis, and planted the seeds for a Jewish future in the United States after World War ll. I began to understand this the day I left for my first conclave in 1951

If we didn't feel a deep sense of community by the time we got off the bus an hour or so later at Camp Alomar in Duchess County, NY, we did by the time we sat down together for a Sabbath meal, replete with candles, *Kiddush, Motzee* and *Birkat HaMazon* (grace after the meal), and above all, the joyful singing of Hebrew and English songs to the accompaniment of guitar.

It was the first time I experienced a real Sabbath meal or, for that matter, a total Sabbath experience. The prayers that evening and on the following morning, perhaps because they were led by us and accompanied by a quickly assembled youth choir, were meaningful. The study sessions led by young rabbis and rabbinical students were engaging as was the singing of Hebrew songs and Israeli dancing. I had never experienced that kind of intense Jewish activity. And the social activities with their group games and programs, all carried out with minimal preparation, gave one a true sense of cohesiveness. When we ended the Sabbath the following night with *Havdallah,* the ceremony that separates the Sabbath from the rest of the week, which I had never witnessed before, I was overtaken with a sense of awe. And when, after another day of non-Sabbath activities which were filled with Jewish content, albeit in an extraordinarily pleasurable way, we packed up to go home, there was, together with all of the happy memories, a sense of melancholy that it was over. The entire ride home was given to making plans for where and when we could come together again. We didn't want to say goodbye.

I returned home filled with a new found sense of my Jewish identity which I had not known in quite the same way. Immediately I began to look forward to the reunions and to returning for a repeat performance a year from then. But, first things first. Not long after I returned home, I began to attend Queens College where my intention was to major in one of the sciences in preparation for admission to dental school. My mother, after all, had been a dental assistant and assured me that dentistry would offer many rewards not the least of which was financial. But she did not have to study chemistry. It did not take long for me to realize that chemistry and I were not going to get along. In addition, on the night of *Yom Kippur* that year, as I lay in bed experiencing pangs of hunger and reflecting on my life, I had this awful vision of having to look down people's open mouths for the rest of my days. I determined then and there that I did not wish to be a dentist.

I did get through chemistry that semester but decided to switch my major to Speech with a minor in education. I had gotten involved with the Q.C. Playshop and landed a leading role in Shakespeare's *A Midsummer*

Night's Dream. Why not acting as a career goal? And if I didn't succeed, I had speech-education to fall back on. After all, teaching was a noble and (in those days) well paying profession. And so it was, until the following fall when I attended my second conclave.

There was a small detour along the way. In a passing conversation with my father about career goals, he mentioned that he had read about a new and up and coming field called Industrial and Labor Relations. While I knew nothing about that field, I learned that a New York State school housed at Cornell University in Ithaca, N.Y. offered a tuition free program in that very field. It just so happened that my best childhood friend Stanley Wyler attended Cornell. Why not take a trip to visit my friend and while there, check on the ILR School and the program it offered? Which is exactly what I did.

It was in March of 1952 that I took the bus to Ithaca and spent a few days visiting with Stanley, attending classes with him, exploring the Cornell campus and checking out the ILR School. I even stopped in at the campus Hillel Foundation. While it was on the Cornell campus, the ILR School was a separate entity, part of the N.Y. State educational system, which explains why it was tuition free. The weather, as I recall, was particularly beautiful and Spring-like. It made the visit most pleasurable and seductive- so much so that when I returned home, I actually filled out the application forms which I had brought back with me and sent them off to Ithaca. I was prepared to forsake Queens College, my parental home and comforts and, for about the same negligible tuition cost (I was paying $7.00 per semester plus the cost of books most of which I could buy in the Used Book Exchange), to attend college on one of the most prestigious campuses in the country. I had only to wait for a positive response which actually did come after Labor Day when a long distance call informed me that I had been accepted. *We would like you to come up,* said a kindly voice on the other end of the line. I could actually become a student at Cornell University.

But the call came too late. The spiritual journey that had begun as I sat next to my maternal grandfather in an orthodox synagogue on 149th St.

in Manhattan was about to take a turn. A day before that long awaited phone call, I had decided that I wanted to become a rabbi. I had returned from my second experience at a GNFTY conclave, this one held at Camp Starlight in Honesdale, PA where I had another marvelously intense Jewish experience. As I shared my enthusiasm upon coming home, my mother, remembering how I had announced my intention to go to Cornell after the return from my prior trip said, in a half mocking fashion: *Now I suppose you'll tell us that you want to become a rabbi?* While, in truth, I hadn't given the matter much thought, the proverbial light bulb suddenly went on and, after a moment's pause, I said: *Yes.* So it was that Cornell lost a student, Industrial and Labor Relations an early pioneer, and I, presumably, a challenging campus experience away from home. But the Jewish People, hopefully, were the beneficiaries of what was to become a wonderful career.

That second Conclave was even better than the first. By now, I had developed some ongoing friendships with boys and girls who had been at the Conclave a year earlier. I was neither a novice nor a stranger. My Jewish I.Q., while still low, had improved somewhat during the year as I found myself beginning to make occasional visits to the Hillel House on campus and to be more aware of the rhythm of Jewish life. Moreover, as one of the older conclavers, I had gained acceptance into the leadership circle, a source of instant respect. It was great for my ego.

All that I had experienced a year earlier-the sense of community, the meaningfulness of daily and Sabbath worship, the dancing and singing of Hebrew songs and the overall intensity of living in a totally Jewish environment twenty four hours each day, even for that brief period of time- was facilitated by a amazing group of young rabbis and rabbinical students. They led the daily discussion groups which we all looked forward to attending and guided us in the manner in which we should lead prayers. They also helped us to prepare the programs and projects that otherwise filled each of those few days. But they did more. They actually played sports with us during the little bit of free time we had and engaged us in conversation about secular as well as religious matters. Altogether, they projected an image totally different from that in our synagogues at home where rabbis seemed stand-offish and aloof. To the contrary, they were regular human beings who were not only religious leaders in the traditional sense but who could joke and laugh and interact on a totally accessible level. It was for me, as they say today, a game-changer.

One rabbi, in particular, was to become a major influence in my life. Herbert Baumgard was then thirty- one years old. I was all of eighteen. He was the rabbi of Temple Bnai Israel in Elmont, Long Island, a new suburban congregation. He had begun to serve it several years earlier while he was still a student at the New York School of the Hebrew Union College-Jewish Institute of Religion, then on West 68th Street in Manhattan. It was the time, after World War II, when there was a marked migration of people, many Jews among them, from the inner city neighborhoods and apartment houses of the five boroughs in which they had grown up to the more spacious, inviting, suburbs of Long Island, Westchester County and New Jersey. There they could smell fresh air and live in a private home with a back yard.

Elmont was a lower middle class neighborhood in Nassau County, a little north of Laurelton but only ten minutes away by car. There were two new synagogues, one Reform and one Conservative across the street from each other. The Reform congregation was committed to Liberal Judaism but was different from mainline Reform congregations in several ways. For one thing, the congregants had chosen to wear *kippot* and *talitot* during worship. For another, they observed the second day of holidays, a custom which almost all Reform Jews had by then forsaken. But the congregation had a sufficient number of members who, while enjoying the idea of being liberal and wanting to affiliate with the Reform Movement rather than the more stringent Conservative Movement, still wanted to maintain their ties to certain more traditional customs. Rabbi Baumgard even appended the traditional *Ameedah* as a supplement to the old *Union Prayer Book* (UPB) so that those who found the shortened version unfulfilling could have an alternative. In that regard, he was very much ahead of his time. The successor to the UPB, the *Gates of Prayer* (GOP) followed that approach by providing many alternative prayer services (ten for Friday night and six for Saturday morning), some more and some less traditional. The most recent Sabbath and weekday prayer book of the Reform Movement, *Mishkan Tefilah* (2007) also provides many options, albeit in yet another format.

Rabbi Baumgard successfully argued, that the essence of Reform was not the rejection of traditional customs but rather the right to make changes in accordance with the needs of a particular community at a particular time. Critical to the process was the idea that those changes were for the purpose of making the tradition more meaningful; not simply for matters of convenience. Moreover, changes could lead one to greater or lesser observance. In a booklet that he published, he showed that the very essence of Judaism was in the ability to change: that the Judaism of the Bible was different from the Judaism of the rabbis which in turn was different from the Judaism of the Middle Ages and so on. From the time Abraham went forth from his father's house to set out for a new land and a new life, Judaism had developed from year to year and from period to period thereby maintaining its vitality.

It was this approach to Reform or Liberal Judaism that was to become the basis of my own philosophy in later years. But let me not get too far ahead of my story. Reform ideology was not yet on my radar in 1952 beyond what I had experienced at the Hebrew Tabernacle, Temple Israel and the conclave. What I had begun to give some thought to, however, was the nature of God. Even before I had made that fated decision to become a rabbi, I was puzzled as to why a supposedly omnipotent and omniscient God would allow evil in the world. It was after all a reflection on God's power, especially after the Holocaust, that innocent people were the object of so much suffering. In the case of the six million who perished during the Holocaust, it seemed there was no reason for their destruction other than that they were Jews. How could this be if God was good and just, the more so if they were God's chosen people?

The question was, of course, not original with me. It had been asked again and again. Perhaps the context was different but the essence was quite the same. While I did not know it then, the biblical book of JOB had dealt with that very issue- what theologians call surd, or inexplicable evil- 2500 years ago. JOB is the story of a righteous man who loses everything, his wealth, his family and his health. When his so-called friends insist that he must have done something to incur God's wrath and urge him to repent, he affirms his innocence and, in a direct challenge not only to his self-proclaimed friends but to the God in whom he believes, he wonders how he can repent when he has in fact done no wrong.

The book thus raises the still unanswered question of why the wicked so often seem to prosper even as the righteous suffer, for no apparent reason. While scholars differ on the meaning of the book, its author seems to be saying two things: First, that simplistic answers such as the underlying premise of the book of DEUTERONOMY, the so called *Deuteronomic Formula* (if you are good you prosper; if you are bad you suffer; if you repent and return to the right path, things will again go well for you) are not sufficient or a true reflection of reality. Second, at the end of the day, one must conclude that finite man simply cannot fathom the ways of God.

But I did not know about the book of JOB then. All I knew was that the God I thought I should believe in seemed capricious and unfair. Moreover, having now had a full year of college, I was beginning to function in a rationalist mode and rationally speaking, I could not believe in a Deity who would have allowed the death of six million if that Diety had the power to prevent it. So I began to think that perhaps there was another approach to the problem of evil in the world. Before I even knew that such an approach might be possible as a legitimate avenue of belief, I began to wonder whether God might be less than all powerful and all knowing. Could one then believe in a God who was imperfect and still be in the Jewish faith community? In a similar vein, I also wondered whether one could be a rabbi if one did not believe in an all powerful God. Wasn't such an affirmation central to the Jewish belief system that one is expected to convey as a rabbi?

At that GNFTY Conclave, I found myself having that conversation with Herbert Baumgard whose teacher, Dr. Henry Slonimsky, five years later to be my teacher, had developed the concept of a *Growing God*. Dean Slonimsky, as he was known, taught that there was the God we wanted there to be, all knowing and all powerful, and the God who is, incomplete and imperfect. Our task as human beings was to give power to the God who is until God becomes the Being we want God to be. *On that day, the Eternal will be One and God's Name will be One*, as the liturgy affirms. When Herbert Baumgard validated my own feelings of discomfort with belief in a perfect God by stating his own belief in a limited God, he not only made possible the decision I was to make when I returned home from the conclave, but provided the basis for what was to be the core of my own God belief in the years to follow until today. While my thinking is a good deal more sophisticated than it was in 1952, it is rooted in the belief that the God I believe in is not a perfect being much as I might wish that God was, and that God needs the individual human being for empowerment as much as we humans need God to make our world more complete.

More of that thinking would emerge during my days in seminary and then as I faced the rigors of daily life as a rabbi. But at the time I decided to pursue the rabbinate, there were other more pressing challenges. How was I to deal with the fact that my Jewish background was so lacking, to the extent that I did not even know the Hebrew alphabet, no less how to read or comprehend our sacred texts or even our prayers? Surely memories of Sunday School studies and the afterglow of two GNFTY conclaves were not enough. I had to start from the very beginning. And I did.

MAKING UP FOR LOST TIME

I arranged for an interview at the New York School of the Hebrew Union College-Jewish Institute of Religion (HUC-JIR) and applied for pre-rabbinic status which would bring with it a draft deferment and the assurance that I could continue my studies uninterrupted. While having played no part in my decision to become a rabbi, it certainly was a side-benefit in those days of the draft when the possibility of being sent to Korea, where we were at war with the North Koreans and Chinese, was very dependent on one's number in the draft lottery.

At the same time, I enrolled in the teacher education program at HUC-JIR which met on Tuesday and Thursday evenings. Twice each week, I took the Long Island Rail Road to New York and then the Subway, followed by a short walk to 40 West 68 St. where I took courses in beginner's Hebrew, Jewish History, Bible and even a course or two in pedagogy. The program was geared to persons seeking a Hebrew School or Religious School teacher's or principal's certificate. The goal was to fill one of the many positions that had become available in the Reform and Conservative synagogues which were sprouting up at a rapid rate in the burgeoning suburban communities of Long Island, Westchester County and New Jersey. Some of the students, as for example, New York City school teachers, were in search of supplementary sources of income. Others were ordinary Jews who, for whatever reason, wanted to become synagogue school teachers. Still others were there to strengthen or, like me, to acquire Jewish backgrounds. It was a unique mix of Jewish souls who sat at the feet of some outstanding Jewish scholars and educators.

During the day, I was carrying a full program at Queens College. On the advice of Rabbi Isaiah Zeldin who interviewed me and who was the

Dean of the New York School of HUC-JIR at the time, I again switched my major, this time from speech to English literature in order to get as broad a Liberal Arts background as possible. I took courses in as wide an array of subjects as I could: in English literature, history, philosophy, sociology and anthropology. Along the way, I also arranged for a required psychiatric interview. When I asked why that was necessary, Rabbi Zeldin opined that one had to be a little *meshuggah* (crazy) to become a rabbi. At the same time, I also continued to pursue my love of acting by taking part in George Bernard Shaw's *Heartbreak House* and in some experimental student productions. I never lost my love for the stage and in later years always harbored a dream of bringing theater into the synagogue. I suppose that in addition to being a little crazy, a rabbi has to be a bit of an actor as well.

As I look back on those college days, I am amazed at how much I was able to get done and how much new information I was able to assimilate. And the learning was not all there was. I also began to put my newfound knowledge to work by teaching religious school. I had begun to work with young people as a youth advisor at Temple Israel of Jamaica, my home congregation, but soon my new found mentor, Herbert Baumgard, invited me to teach for him in Elmont, LI., only fifteen minutes or so from home. It was there that I had some of the happiest and most formative teaching experiences of my life. The children were young, unspoiled and eager to learn. I was inexperienced, but filled with enthusiasm, and a desire to share what I was discovering and growing to love about Judaism even though I had only the most rudimentary pedagogic background. But I did have a good instinct for how to transmit learning and to make it fun. I taught second and third graders who were a delight and seventh and eighth graders who were a bit more challenging but also responsive. I have often thought back to those early years. At a much later time, I learned that many of my forebears were Jewish teachers. So perhaps there is some truth in the old adage that apples do not fall far from trees.

I referred to the fact that I trace much of my approach to Reform Judaism to my Elmont experience and, in particular, to Rabbi Baumgard, so I should add that it was here that I had, really, my first encounter with *kipah* and *talit*. Having grown up in what can best be described as a Classical Reform Congregation where there was minimal use of Hebrew in the service and music that was akin to melodies you might hear at a Sunday Service in a Protestant Church, I did not witness anyone wearing a *yarmulke* on his head or a *talit* around the shoulders. I had a vague recollection of seeing such things in the synagogue in Manhattan I had attended with my grandfather but nothing in more recent history; not even at conclave. But here in Elmont, at Congregation B'nai Israel, men and boys were required to cover their heads in prayer, even in Hebrew school. That was a new experience for me. And I liked it. I remember the day I first wore a *talit* at a Sabbath morning service. At that time I didn't know the source in NUMBERS 15:37-41 where we are commanded to *wear fringes on the corners of (y)our garments…*but I remember experiencing a sense of great warmth and feeling very special when I wrapped myself in the prayer shawl. It is a feeling and a memory that recurs until today. How true the words of the Israeli poet Yehudah Amichai, *whoever wrapped himself in a talit when he was young will never forget.*

To that point, I had understood the reform in Reform Judaism to refer to the things we did not do, e.g. pray with hats, keep kosher, observe second days of holidays and the like. Now I was beginning to understand that being a Reform Jew could also mean choosing to observe old customs and traditions once discarded and to discover in them new relevance. What made us Reform was not that we were rejectionist but that we sought to infuse what we do with meaning and that we looked for ways of deepening our Jewish commitment. While I did not realize it then, it was a theme that I would have occasion to return to many times, especially during the early years of my rabbinate as I sought to interpret what I understood as the new direction in which the Reform Movement was moving. What I did realize is that, while I still lagged far behind where I would have liked to have been, my Jewish I.Q. was definitely on the rise. The teaching experience was to stand me in good stead in later years.

OTHER INFLUENCES

It was during that period, I also began to be involved at the Hillel Foundation of Queens College, where I came to know two rabbis who welcomed me into the new Jewish world that I was discovering. Hillel, the Jewish Student's organization which, in those days, was sponsored and supported financially by B'nai Brith, was situated in an off-campus house to which we students who were interested in things Jewish and also were not averse to meeting potential dating partners, would come to hang out between classes and to participate in programs. Rabbi Maurice Schatz, a Reform rabbi who had been a student of the great Rabbi Stephen S. Wise, founder of the Jewish Institute of Religion, the seminary I was to attend, was its director at the time I entered Q.C. He was a kind man whom I liked, but he left after my sophomore year to assume a pulpit.

Perhaps it was fortuitous for it was his replacement, Rabbi Saul Kraft, who opened my eyes to yet another view within what I was discovering to be the vast spectrum of Jewish thought. While having been ordained at the Conservative Jewish Theological Seminary (JTS), he was a Reconstructionist; a disciple of Rabbi Mordecai Kaplan. It took me longer than my few years at Hillel to get a handle on just what Reconstructionists believed but it was clear that while he was ritually observant, Rabbi Kraft was quite radical theologically. It was a combination that intrigued me because it would eventually be the exact place that I would one day find myself. I subsequently maintained contact with him for many years and was delighted when, much later, we met once again during the summers that we both spent listening to classical music at Tanglewood, summer home of the Boston Symphony Orchestra, in the Berkshire Hills of Massachusetts.

I have two particularly vivid memories from those earlier days. The one is of a discussion of the sexiest book in the Bible, THE SONG OF SONGS, about which I knew nothing at the time but which Saul Kraft brought to life in his inimitable way. Traditionalists describe it as an allegory depicting God's love for Israel. Saul Kraft stressed that it was out and out love poetry, challenging the Orthodox approach and stressing instead its human aspect. I did not know until then that one, especially a rabbi, could approach a biblical text in so irreverent a way. Nor did I understand how such an obviously erotic collection of poetry could actually have been admitted into the Hebrew Bible. Yet, no less an ancient sage than the great Rabbi Akiba had said that *while all of the Writings* (the third division of the Hebrew Bible) *are holy, the SONG OF SONGS is the Holy of Holies.* His opinion was so highly regarded that this unlikely book was admitted to the biblical cannon, another example of the brilliance and daring of our forebears.

In later years, I grew increasingly fond of that text and made sure always to read from it and to have its words sung during services on the Sabbath between the first and last day of Passover, when the tradition calls for it to be read publicly. Springtime was after all not only a time for freedom and rebirth, the themes of Passover. It was also a time when, as the poet said, *a young man's fancy turns to thoughts of love.* That our Tradition found a way to integrate all three themes by ritualizing the public reading of a controversial book is yet one more example of its genius.

My other memory involving Rabbi Kraft during those Queens College days is instructive in a different way. We Hillel students were invited to a Shabbat gathering at the Kraft home on a certain Friday night. Rabbi Kraft, true to the biblical prohibition against making a fire on the Sabbath, asked that we not smoke. But how could it be that one so seemingly irreverent when it came to the Bible, our most sacred text, could be so old fashioned when it came to observance? Why would he place so seemingly onerous a restriction on those of us who were not committed to the laws of the Sabbath of which we were largely ignorant in any case? So, to my everlasting regret and shame, I lit up (I smoked in those days). Only later did I understand that that I should have followed the rules of the host in whose home I was a guest and for whom not smoking was a meaningful tradition even though, it may have been for reasons other than observance of the literal meaning of the biblical prohibition per se. Moreover there were those who were offended by my action including not only Rabbi Kraft but others who were equally or perhaps even more observant.

It was a lesson that did not register on that particular night but one that is important to learn, especially for the younger generation to which I once belonged (as did we all), namely: there are times when one needs to put his or her own desires aside, especially if it is only for a short time, in order to be respectful of the feelings and needs of others. But more, it was also an illustration of how one can be a free spirit intellectually in terms of one's belief system yet find meaning in custom and tradition even when it might not seem totally rational. While what we do should not defy the laws of reason, it need not always adhere to them. There is, I believe, a subtle difference. Over the years, I have come to understand that the need to be sensitive to the beliefs and practices of others when in their presence should, in most cases, trump one's personal preferences. There is nothing to be gained by flaunting one's liberalism while in the presence of those who are strict in their observance of the tradition.

With the passage of time, I discovered another dimension to the issue of smoking on the Sabbath that is helpful in shedding light on the unique approach of Reform Judaism to matters of Jewish practice. Few Liberal Jews understand the biblical injunction against making a fire to apply to their lives in the way that Orthodox Jews do. Not turning on the stove even if it is electric, not switching on the lights or the TV nor driving a car or even using a microphone because each of those acts creates a spark and is therefore akin to making a fire does not resonate in the mind of the Liberal Jew. But what of the more basic question: to smoke on the Sabbath; or not? Not smoking, after all, had long been considered the norm in Jewish life, whatever the reason. Should it not then carry some weight?

Here is where the great strength and at the same time weakness, or perhaps better, challenge of Reform comes to bare. Unlike Orthodoxy which operates within a clearly- defined authoritative system, Reform Judaism, by its very nature, provides no definitive answer to the question, no command from on high. It relies rather on informed choice based upon knowledge of traditional norms as well as a response to contemporary needs all within the bounds of reason.

Of course, while today, given the general aversion to smoking, the matter is somewhat academic, at an earlier time, the matter was ripe for debate in certain circles and provides a valuable insight into the nature of Reform Judaism and the thinking of its adherents. Even though no one within the family of Reform Judaism found the command to not make a fire on the Sabbath binding in the same way as was, for example, not eating bread on *Pesach*, the question of whether or not to smoke on the Sabbath could become a lively topic of discussion among those who wanted to apply Jewish values to their lives.

There were those who argued that since the essence of the Sabbath is that it should be a day of joy (*oneg*), if smoking on the Sabbath, brought one special joy, it should not only be permitted but it should be embraced. Conversely, there were others who argued that since what makes the Sabbath most special (holy) is found in its being different from the rest of the workaday week, if one smoked during six days of the week, one should abstain on the seventh day, not because of the prohibition against making a fire but in order to give the day special significance.

Using that line of reasoning, there were also those who argued that a person who did not smoke regularly might take great delight in lighting up after a Sabbath meal. And so it went. As I came to understand more about Reform Judaism, I came to realize that at its best, it was not about making the most convenient choice but coming to the best reasoned choice. After a sincere search, *the tradition*, as one of the great Reform legalists who also left his mark on my thinking, Rabbi Dr. Solomon Freehoff, taught, *has a vote but not a veto.*

On a personal note, even while I still smoked, I came to find the idea of not smoking on Shabbat quite compelling. It heightened my self-awareness as a Jew and gave special meaning to the day. In that context, I was especially moved by a story recounted in his book *The Sabbath* by Rabbi Abraham Joshuah Heschel, another of the great thinkers and teachers of the twentieth century. He tells of the Jew who was locked in a windowless cell in a Russian prison and thus unable to tell night from day or to know the passage of the time. But this observant Jew who had been a compulsive smoker was able to keep time because on every seventh day he lost the urge to smoke. His inner clock told him it was the Sabbath, the day made special by the fact that he did not smoke. And so despite the terrible circumstances of his incarceration, he never lost sight of who he was and where he was both in space and time.

I am especially fond of that story because it demonstrates so well the power of our tradition. But it stresses too that what matters at least as much as the letter of the law is its spirit and how it helps to shape our lives. And that, I came to discover, is what is really at the heart of Reform Judaism.

A BRIEF BUT IMPORTANT BY-WAY

B etween the pursuit of my academic studies at Queens College, attendance at evening pre-rabbinic classes and teaching for Rabbi Baumgard at Bnai Israel in Elmont, my days were full, although I did not give up on my love of acting entirely. I continued to be involved with the Q.C. Playshop as well. But now, I chose English literature as my major for it provided me with a jumping off point from which I could venture into other subjects like philosophy, sociology and history beyond the two year language, literature and arts curriculum (akin to that taught at Columbia University) required of everyone attending any of the City Colleges in New York. I had been advised to get as broad a liberal arts education as was possible for this would benefit me in later years, providing me with a solid fundamental education. This is exactly the course I followed. Jewish subjects (beyond essential tools, such as knowledge of Hebrew) would come later.

Quite naturally I seized upon other opportunities that would broaden my outlook and better prepare me for what was to lie in store in the years to come. One such opportunity was to make a strong impression on me and to profoundly shape my value system. Through the Hillel Foundation, I learned that the National Conference of Christians and Jews, an organization devoted to fostering interfaith understanding through dialogue, was holding a human relations workshop for college students at an away campsite at the end of the school year in June. Sensing that both a learning experience as well as a social experience lay in store for me and armed with the knowledge that scholarships were available, I applied and was consequently accepted. The experience was extraordinary.

Thirty or forty young men and women, representing the three major faiths (Moslems were not then a presence) and coming from colleges around Greater New York, spent the weekend in conversation with each other. Using Psycho Drama, Socio Drama and other human relations tools, all under the guidance of trained facilitators, we focused on the causes of prejudice and explored those things which separated us even as we discovered how much we had in common. The instructors and counselors, some of whom were part of the NCCJ structure while others were professors at local universities, were totally accessible and forthcoming. By the end of those several days, they had helped us discover that being different from each other did not have to lead to distrust or denigration of another person; that people of different faiths and backgrounds could function beautifully together without anyone giving up his or her own uniqueness. In a sense, we learned that messianic dreams of peace and understanding between people and nations could be realized given the proper environment.

That lesson became even more apparent at the end of the summer at a similar conference, this time for high school students. Grace Macarone, a Catholic young woman, and I, who had been at the college conference, were invited to return and to serve as counselors. These students were all from New York City high schools. Not only did they have different religious faiths, but they came from a wide range of socio- economic backgrounds including some from rough neighborhoods. Still, the end result was the same. They were able to get along and, in a short time, had learned to respect each other for who they were. What they had most in common was precisely that they were different. One of the most poignant and lasting moments of that conference was during our closing friendship circle. A young gang leader who somehow had managed to escape from his environment for these few days but knew he had to go back home to the gang said, with tears in his eyes: *How will I be able to explain to the others what we have been able to create during these few days? If only I could recreate this experience at home, how much better it would be for us all.*

Sadly, NCCJ no longer exists in the way it did then. But I remain forever indebted to the role it played in my spiritual journey. It taught me, other indications to the contrary, that efforts to reach out to those who are different from us are worthwhile and can only enrich the human condition. To dream, as did Isaiah, of a time when *the wolf will lie down with the lamb, the leopard…with the kid,* need not be in vain. To allow cynicism to overtake hopefulness is little more than a self fulfilling prophecy. More important is it for us to affirm the words of Malachai: *Have we not one Father; Has not one God created us?* During my remaining years at Queens College, I tried to convey that message in my daily life and at the special NCCJ sponsored events to which I was invited. At one of them, incidentally, I had the privilege of sitting next to and chatting with the iconic Jackie Robinson, who was one of those special human beings whom one does not easily forget. One of my prized possessions from those days which still sits on my book shelf is a plaque presented to me by the Dead End Boys, a Queens College fraternity, *for leadership and inspiration in promoting the ideals of Brotherhood.*

My college years, then, were years of discovery, not only of the vast world of knowledge of which I had the opportunity to taste only a smattering during my four years as an undergraduate but of the world of Jewish life into which I had only recently begun to enter in a serious way. It was also my introduction into the larger universe of which I was a part. I had after all, grown up in a somewhat sheltered environment, the only child of European parents who in their zeal to create a new life for themselves and for me, had protected me from the temptations of the real world. Early curfews even into high school and other restrictions had kept me from becoming very socially active or popular. It was only now that I began to see the world with different eyes. I grew up during the four years at Queens College. They came to an end, all too quickly. I remember wishing, during graduation, that I could now begin my studies for I realized how little I knew and how much there was to be learned. But the reality was that I was now ready for the next step on my journey, entry into the New York School of the Hebrew Union College-Jewish Institute of Religion as a full time rabbinic student.

THE SEMINARY YEARS

Well, almost ready. Despite diligent study for three years in the HUC-JIR School of Education, I along with other rabbinic candidates was still deficient in my Hebrew language capability. An hour of Hebrew twice a week is just not enough. The Seminary recognized that and created a summer program for those of us (most of the entering class) who needed further tutelage prior to beginning their full time studies. It did so by creating a summer pre-rabbinic program at an estate which was bequeathed to it in Towanda, PA, on the banks of the Susquehanna River. There for seven weeks, we gathered and lived, ate, played, prayed and studied together with senior rabbinic students who taught us together with faculty of the Hebrew Union College. Like the GNFTY conclaves, it was another complete Jewish experience in the sense that we were immersed in a Jewish environment twenty-four hours a day. Only here, unlike the Conclave which was a social experience, the goal was purely to learn with the emphasis being on Hebrew. We were divided into groups depending on our ability. Most of us were pretty much at the beginner's level. But over the weeks, we progressed sufficiently so that some of us were able to pass off the basic grammar course that was required of all first year seminarians.

Having first gone to Towanda before beginning my senior year of college, I was able to benefit from two summers in the pre-rabbinic camp program: one before my senior year and a second after I graduated from college. What made the program special was not only the intensive learning (we studied Hebrew texts and Hebrew grammar) but also the opportunity to participate in daily prayer, morning and evening. We each had opportunities to lead services and to give brief sermons. We interacted not only with each other but with visiting professors and with prominent pulpit rabbis who stopped by to visit and to share their scholarship and experience. In retrospect, however, the program, valuable as it was, fell short because it did not immerse us in the spoken language which would have given us a much better grounding in Hebrew than learning how to parse verbs in seven declensions. But modern Hebrew had historically not been stressed in the Cincinnati school of HUC-JIR. In fact, during the heyday of so called Classical Reform Judaism, it was not even part of the curriculum. The rebirth of Israel would, of course, change that. But even so, it would not be until 1970 that all new rabbinical students were required to spend their first year in Israel learning the language. Would that I might have had that opportunity! While I was awarded a modern Hebrew prize upon being ordained, it was much more for progress than for ability. The fact is my spoken Hebrew was never very good. To this day, that is one of my great regrets.

What I did discover in Towanda was Shabbat. Not the Shabbat my forebears observed which centered on what one was not to do: turn on light bulbs or use electronic devices, light a match, cook a meal, drive a car (all the things derived from the biblical prohibition against making a fire), write more than two letters of the alphabet or sew (no creating anything new), work and a host of prohibitions which might easily cause Shabbat to be viewed as little more than a day of don'ts. Rather Shabbat became for me, indeed for all of us, what I truly believe it is meant to be: a cessation for a day from all that one is engaged in during the other six days. We tried to do what would make the day different from the rest of the week; what would be *kodesh* (holy) as opposed to *chol* (ordinary).

Here is how it played out. On Friday afternoon, we stopped our studies and cleaned up the campus and ourselves, showering and shaving and wearing a nice clean shirt and slacks instead of a T-shirt and shorts (we were of course only men in those days), our weekday attire. Dinner was more elaborate, served on a white tablecloth. There were candles and wine and *Challah*. Of course we gathered to greet the *Sabbath Bride* with our prayers and songs. The entire evening was festive and was a welcome break from the other days. But it did not end on Friday night. Saturday morning there were again services with Torah reading and sermon, delivered by our guest if there was one that week. After prayers, we played volleyball, a great diversion, and then had lunch. The afternoon was completely free. We each spent it by doing something special. I used to love to listen to the opera on Saturday afternoon and also to use the time to write home to my parents and friends or to read a book just for fun. When the day ended in the evening, we ushered out the day with the service of separation called *Havdallah*, somewhat wistfully, for it meant returning to the task at hand which was our studies.

Normally, studying is a very appropriate activity for the Sabbath. But for us it was our *work* and so it was the one thing we did not do, thus making the day different from the other days of the week. Does that fit the Orthodox definition of Shabbat? Certainly not in a literal way. But that is precisely what Reform Judaism is all about: an effort to bring new meaning to old beliefs and practices thereby capturing the spirit of the law even when it means sometimes violating the letter. The Sabbath experience in Towanda became the model for me throughout the years. I still love to listen to the opera and to just read for fun on Saturday afternoon. Of course, in retirement, there are many more opportunities for leisure time activities; but Shabbat remains a special day.

Perhaps a word is in order about the seminary I entered after my second summer in Towanda and how it got such a long name. The Hebrew Union College in Cincinnati was founded in 1875 by Rabbi Isaac Mayer Wise to train English speaking rabbis to become leaders of American synagogues. Wise had a dream of creating an Americanized form of Judaism as opposed to forms that were rooted in the traditions and style of Eastern Europe. He had not intended to reject Judaism or even to revolutionize it; just to make it compatible with the American rather than the European style of life. Thus he created a consortium of congregations that he called the Union of American Hebrew Congregations. He used *Hebrew* rather than *Jewish* because that struck him as being more acceptable to the American Christian population which understood that they themselves were rooted in the civilization of the ancient Hebrews.

The very nature of the Hebrew Union College was such, however, that it led to changes that became known as Reform Judaism, an expression of Judaism that, over the years, moved farther and farther away from historical Jewish tradition. The point when, in the eyes of another segment of the Jewish population, reforms such as not requiring adherence to the Dietary Laws (*Kashrut*), doing away with head coverings and prayer shawls, minimizing the use of Hebrew in the prayer service and rejecting belief in a personal messiah, among others, became too extreme, Conservative Judaism was born. It saw itself as a way to put the brakes on change; to *conserve* Judaism before it became devoid of its central principles and customs.

Since the focus of Reform was on adapting to the new American environment, there was also a de-emphasis on all that had to do with the desire for a return to Zion, so long perceived as the homeland of the Jewish People. After all, the argument went, the U.S.A. was our Promised Land, Washington (or Charleston, S.C. or Savannah, GA) was our Jerusalem, and whatever synagogue we attended was our Temple. So prayers for the return to Zion were excised from the prayer book along with prayers for the restoration of the Temple in Jerusalem and its accompanying animal sacrifices. Any political activity directed to the re-establishment of a Jewish homeland or any identification with Zionist activity were considered at best unnecessary or at worst, antithetical to the aims of Reform Judaism.

But the world had changed by the second decade of the twentieth century, especially the Jewish world, and was, of course, to change even more radically in the 30s and 40s. There were Liberal rabbis who understood the need for Judaism to adapt to its new surroundings and new found freedoms. They also understood that there could be no complete Jewish expression without a relationship to the land in which our people was born; where Jews who wanted to live a complete Jewish life could be free from anti-Semitism. Among them was another Wise, Stephen Samuel by name.

Isaac Mayer Wise was known as the architect of American Reform Judaism, the master builder of the first indigenously created institutions of American Jewish life (not only the Hebrew Union College but the Union of American Hebrew Congregations, today called the Union for Reform Judaism or URJ). Stephen Samuel Wise gained fame as a charismatic preacher and a prophetic voice that called for integrity in government and advocated for the oppressed and persecuted, Jew and non-Jew alike. He was also an ardent Zionist, who in 1898 attended the Second Zionist Congress in Basle, Switzerland and supported Theodore Herzl in his call for a Jewish state in direct opposition to Isaac M. Wise who was critical of Herzl.

Sensing a need for a seminary to train rabbis who were not ideologically bound to a particular stream of Jewish life even though he himself was committed to Reform, and where Zionism would not be a dirty word, Wise created the Jewish Institute of Religion in New York City in 1922. What made the JIR unique was the fact that, while it was unquestionably a Liberal seminary, students were able to choose in what stream of Judaism they wanted to serve upon ordination. In point of fact, while most of the graduates of JIR were to serve Reform pulpits, a number of very prominent graduates of the school served Conservative and in a few cases, even Orthodox pulpits. Perhaps most interesting for those of us who are South Floridians is the fact that both the late Leon Kronish and Irving Lehrman were ordained by Stephen Wise in 1942 and both became leading Rabbis on Miami Beach: Kronish in the Reform (he called it Liberal) Temple Beth Shalom; Lehrman at the Conservative Temple Emanuel. And both it should be added were among the leading Zionists of their generation thanks undoubtedly, at least in part, to their training at JIR. While I could have attended either the Cincinnati or New York branch of the HUC-JIR, I decided on the New York school and began my studies there in the fall of 1955.

There were a number of reasons for my decision. The two summers that I had spent in Towanda gave me a sense of what living in the dorm at HUC in Cincinnati might be like: a closed in environment with a group of men all of whom shared the same professional objective thus not allowing for (at least to my way of thinking) a variety of broadening experiences. Moreover, I sensed a degree of rigidity in the academic approach on the part of the faculty members whom I encountered which was antithetical to the kind of openness to which I was accustomed. And Cincinnati was after all a small Midwestern town while I was a New Yorker. New York would allow me many more opportunities to grow intellectually and socially and could also provide me more chances to earn money. There were numerous synagogues that needed Sunday school and Hebrew school teachers, positions often filled by rabbinical students, not to speak of new congregations which were springing up in and around New York City. They engaged student rabbis to serve them until they were ready to engage a full time rabbi. Finally, there was the advice I received from my mentor Herbert Baumgard who extolled the New York School for its open intellectual atmosphere, the quality of its eclectic faculty and the liberal, non doctrinaire ideology which pervaded its halls.

My expectations were fullfilled. The five years I spent at the New York School of the Hebrew Union College-Jewish Institute of Religion provided me with the foundation blocks which were to serve as the basis of my life as a rabbi. While my two summers in Towanda enabled me to "pass off" biblical grammar, just about everything else was new to me. We were thrown into Hebrew texts: Bible with *Rashi, Midrash, Mishna* and modern literature. Later we would be introduced to *Talmud*, codes, philosophy, Jewish thought and history. We studied Jewish music learning *Torah* and *Haftarah* trope and the main melodies we were expected to sing in our student pulpits, as well as speech and homiletics. After all the ability to orate well was as important to success in the pulpit as was scholarship. A course in human relations taught us how to deal with congregants in public and private settings; when to engage in short term counseling and when to refer people to mental health professionals.

For me, it was all new-- a time of self discovery and the beginning of a continuing love affair with the wondrous way of life we know as Judaism: filled with rules and traditions yet open to development and change; established on faith yet grounded in a rational approach which led to never ending challenges to the tradition, not only by students, my classmates, but by professors who were lovers of Zion even as they exuded a critical if not even, at times, cynical demeanor.

From the fifteen who signed my *Semicha* (Certificate of Ordination), I mention four who were especially influential. Dr. Harry M. Orlinsky, one of the world's great Bible scholars, was my baseball-loving Bible professor and became my thesis advisor under whom I analyzed and critiqued the Buber-Rosenzweig translation of *Genesis* (accepted with honors). Martin Buber and Franz Rosenzweig were German Jewish existential thinkers who, in addition to their philosophical writings, created an important Jewish learning institution in the early part of the twentieth century in Frankfurt called The *Lehrhaus* (The Learning Place). German Jews with widely varying degrees of Jewish knowledge came there to study and to strengthen their ties to Jewish life. When I established an adult education Program at Temple Sinai many years later, I called it the *Lehrhaus* as an *homage* to them.

But equal renown came to them for what became known as the *Buber Rosenzweig Bible*, the methodology of which I studied under the guidance of Dr. Orlinsky. They sought to translate the Hebrew Bible into an ancient classical form of German so that the German speaking reader in the 1920s might experience the text in a manner akin to the way the Hebrew-literate Jew experienced the text when he read or heard the original. Put another way, they tried to transform the ancient Hebrew with all of its literary nuances, poetry and wordplay into German while retaining the literal meaning of the text at the same time. It was a brilliant effort but one that I concluded was a glorious failure for as any student of translation will attest, one cannot turn one language into another, as they tried to do. Rosenzweig himself had famously pointed out that *all translation is interpretation.*

I take this little detour into the realm of biblical translation not only because of my thesis but because, at the very time we were students at HUC-JIR, Dr. Orlinsky, affectionately referred to as HMO, was, the chairman of the Jewish Publication Society committee which was engaged in translating the Torah into modern English. In contrast to the methodology of Buber- Rosenzweig, the goal of the JPS committee was to render the ancient biblical text in a modern, colloquial English, that was easily comprehensible while being accurate in its meaning, reflective of the latest and best in scholarship. It was no easy task. The project would not be complete until two years after I was ordained. The work of translating the rest of the Hebrew Bible would continue for twenty plus years into the 1980s under several different committees of translators and would not be ready for publication until 1985 when it finally replaced the earlier 1917 version.

From HMO I learned that one needed to read meaning *out of the text (exegesis)*, not *into the text (eisegesis)* as so many of the so called *higher critics* of the Bible were wont to do. Christian scholars especially, were fond of using the Hebrew Bible to justify their particular religious bias. That is, they made the text mean what, for their own reasons, they wanted it to mean, even if it was contrary to the real meaning. For example, they mistranslated the word *Almah* (young woman) in *ISAIAH 7:14 (an almah shall conceive and bear a child)* to be *virgin* even though the Hebrew word for virgin is clearly *betulah*. Thus they could claim that Isaiah, in the eighth century BCE, was forecasting the birth of Jesus, whom they claimed was born of a virgin. Not only, Dr. Orlinsky argued, could Isaiah, who lived 800 years before Jesus, not have known of his birth, but this was a blatant reading into the text rather than reading what was there: a clear example of *eisegesis*.

The Bible professors at the Cincinnati Branch of HUC-JIR were also not guiltless. They frequently would emend a difficult text to give it more coherence and to make it mean what they wanted it to mean even when the text was far from clear. Dr. Orlinsky took the text at face value. It was important to him that one not try to make the text say what it does not say when translating for while that might make for good theology or comprehension it did not make for good scholarship. That today's biblical scholars take the biblical text as it is written far more seriously than did an earlier generation of scholars who took liberties with it when they thought it was corrupt, is due in significant measure to the work of Dr. Orlinsky.

Equally impressive but in a very different way, Rabbi Dr. John Tepfer, an urbane Englishman with a cutting sense of humor, introduced us to rabbinic texts and the history of the Talmudic Period. He taught that Jewish Law did not develop in a vacuum but in a historical setting, and needed to be understood in context. His theory that the famous *Pirke Avot* (*Chapters* or *Sayings of the Fathers*) was a collection of instructions to those who were the heads of Courts of Law, each an *Av Beit Din,* still buzzes around in my head whenever I come in contact with that ancient section of the *Mishna*. An important part of our legal literature, it appears in many prayer books and is studied during the weeks between *Pesach* and *Shavuot*. I often quote from its wisdom.

In addition to what he offered in the classroom, Dr. Tepfer critiqued the sermon of the student preacher during Chapel each Friday, sometimes mercilessly. We dreaded that encounter. However we did become better preachers as a result.

But most compelling was an elective on the origins and nature of *Hasidim* as it developed in the late eighteenth century. Dr. Tepfer reframed what is today commonly viewed as an extreme form of Orthodoxy, as a kind of Reform Movement that rose up against an aristocracy of learning that existed among the wealthy who, unlike the hard working poor, had leisure time to study. Thus only they could lay claim to piety in accordance with a rabbinic saying that *an ignorant man cannot be pious*. Dramatically, the founder of *Hasidism, the Baal Shem Tov* (Master of the good Name) stressed that the less- learned poor could also find favor in God's eyes. They could give expression to their yearnings with joy even if without knowledge, through the telling of stories, dance and melodies without words.

Despite the fact that the *Hasidism* we encounter today would seem to be far removed from the vision of its early masters and inimical to much I hold dear, I find myself very much attracted to the idea that Jewish worship should be joyful and spontaneous. I came to realize that while Reform Judaism brought a certain discipline and decorum back into the synagogue in its earlier days, it also helped to create an environment that was oftentimes cold, sterile and without spirit. One of the goals I set for myself during my seminary days was to bring back some of the joy that was missing. I would reintroduce rituals long ignored by Reform such as *Selichot* (prayers of forgiveness) at midnight on the Saturday before *Rosh Hashanah* and *Havdalah* at the end of the Sabbath, both with perhaps a touch of the mystical which was also the mark of *Hasidism*. Even more critical was it to reintroduce authentically Jewish music that would encourage singing and participation by the congregation and, at times, even spontaneous dance. Whatever success I had in later years in pursuit of that goal was in some measure the result of Dr. Tepfer's course.

In contrast to the urbanity of Dr. Tepfer was Professor Samuel Atlas who, used to jokingly refer to himself as *the dash in HUC – JIR* because he taught both in New York and Cincinnati (a semester in the one, a semester in the other). In his thick *Yiddish* accent, he taught us Jewish philosophy and Talmud with a rationalist slant. He had been reared in and steeped in the old East European Yeshiva world and could quote from the entire Talmud by heart, even as he was an expert in Kantian philosophy, an exponent of what he called *critical idealism*. For him the greatness of the Talmud was that it was grounded in an ethical value system. The ancient rabbis did not hesitate to overturn Torah law when they felt it was for the greater good of their society as for example when Hillel issued his famous *Prosbul* which enabled commerce to continue during the seventh or Sabbatical year when all debts where to have been cancelled, by transferring them instead to a *Beit Din* (Law Court). It was that brilliantly-conceived legal fiction which allowed lenders to continue lending and borrowers to continue borrowing. The times, after all had changed so that the biblical law which had once upon a time protected the poor in an agrarian society now worked against them in the new world of commerce which depended on borrowing and lending. Hillel understood as another Talmudic principle put it, that in a time of emergency (*Et laasot ladonai-a time to do for God*) we (even) overturn the Torah (*heyfeiru Toratecha*).

When it came to philosophy and intellectual discourse, Dr. Atlas could not abide ignorance or the American view that everyone has a right to an opinion and that each person's opinion, whether grounded in knowledge or not, is of equal worth. He loathed what he referred to as a *shallow relativism* in which *this one is right and that one is right*. From him I learned what was to become my approach to Reform Judaism: First, if the essence of reform has to do with making choices, one needs to make Jewish choices based on Jewish knowledge and not on convenience or what is the easiest path to follow lest we end up with a minimalist Judaism: a kind of Judaism Lite. Assuredly, the opinion of someone who has no Jewish learning or minimal learning, while it may be sincere, should not carry the same weight as that of someone who has studied the sources. Second, that if Reform Judaism is not to become frozen in its development we need to understand, as Dr. Atlas taught, that there are only two types of Jews who transcend the labels which normally identify the streams of Jewish life. There are Philosophical Jews and Dogmatic Jews: those whose behavior results from an *we have always done it this way* approach, and those who arrive at decisions after careful and measured thought. Dr. Atlas, of course, favored Philosophical Jews but taught that there are examples of both, in the world of Orthodoxy as well as the world of Reform.

In Orthodoxy, there are dogmatists who unthinkingly abjure any departure from what has gone on before and resist all accommodation to modernism or the legitimacy of alternative points of view. But there are also rational modernists who are open to new ideas even as they remain strict in their commitment to Jewish Law and who accept that there are expressions of Judaism other than their own. One can sit at the table with them and engage in meaningful discussion.

Similarly, there are Reform Jews who have become so set in their tradition-denying ways that their *Reform* becomes unchanging and rigid, thus as dogmatic as that of the most extremely Orthodox. But there are also Reform Jews whose thinking leads them to be open to exploring new ways of bringing long forgotten traditions back into their lives; not because anyone is forcing them to but because they choose to and because it is helpful in their search for a more meaningful expression of Jewish life.

I often found myself quoting Dr. Atlas to congregants who were stuck in their ways and unthinkingly saw any change towards tradition as a return to Orthodoxy, for example, the wearing of a *talit* or *kipah* or the addition of a second day of *Rosh Hashanah* which Reform Judaism had once forsworn. During such times I tried to explain that the essence of Reform Judaism, as I had come to understand it, lay in its way of affirming non- dogmatism and rationality. I was, I believe, able to do so with some success. No wonder we lovingly referred to Dr. Atlas as *Charlie,* after the body builder Charles Atlas, because while he was just the opposite- short and pudgy- he was a powerhouse, a giant in his way.

The last of the four, all of whom have long since gone to the Yeshiva on High, was already retired when I began my years as a student. But thankfully he was allowed to offer electives and some of us had the benefit of sitting at his feet. That was Dr. Henry Slonimsky whom I mentioned above in another context. To be in his class was to be in the presence of an overpowering personality who had the charisma and passion of a biblical prophet. No matter the subject, whether the inspiring words of the prophet Jeremiah, the birth and death of Jesus- for him a prototype of Jewish suffering (*a Jew has to suffer* he would say) -or the writings of Dostoyevsky, every lecture was like a sermon, delivered with zeal as if from Mt. Sinai. For him there was no greater volume of Jewish literature than the prayer book (a repository of the best of Jewish thinking through the ages) or greater imperative than to love Jews, God's chosen, with all of their flaws. He viewed Mordecai Kaplan, the founder of Reconstructionism, with disdain, precisely because he disavowed choseness.

Dr. Slonimsky studied with the great German Jewish philosopher Herman Cohen in Marburg, Germany and earned a PHD although he never became a rabbi. When we met him he had a shock of thinning white hair and was already well on in years. But his voice still boomed as it had in his younger days when Stephen Wise first tapped him to be on the faculty of JIR. He would say to us that a rabbi has but one sermon which he preaches throughout his lifetime with variations on a theme – an observation which probably is not far off the mark as I reflect back on the years of my own rabbinate. In my final *Kol Nidre* sermon at Temple Sinai, preached on the eve of my retirement in 1997, I tried to capture that *one sermon* with the words *Do Jewish*, for that is the message I tried to convey in a myriad ways throughout my years in the pulpit.

In like manner, everything that Dr. Slonimsky taught grew out of his singular concept of the *growing* God, to which I alluded above but which bears repeating. His conviction was that God gains strength as man gains strength. It was our task as human beings to empower God so that at the end of time, the God we idealize and want to have power and the God who exists in reality but is at present limited will become the same. That was the goal of history. I think of Dr. Slonimsky each time we come to the end of the *Aleynu* prayer and sing *on that day the Eternal will be One and God's Name will be One* for that in essence was his proof text.

As I reflect on those long-ago years and those wonderful teachers who along with others that I do not name here were so influential in moving me along on my spiritual journey, I am amazed at how much was thrown at us and even more, how much we managed to absorb and get done. Keep in mind that even as we were full time students, we had jobs as Sunday school and Hebrew school teachers and administrators and, then, beginning in our second year (some actually in their first year), as student rabbis in the rapidly growing landscape of new synagogues that were springing up in the suburbs of New York and New Jersey in the 1950s. Those newly formed congregations were still too small to afford full time rabbis, even if there had been enough rabbis to go around, so they engaged seminarians to conduct services and to head their education programs. The very fact that we were attending rabbinical school brought with it the assumption that we knew what we were doing. Fortunately, little did they know how little we knew, and who were we to burst that bubble? But somehow it worked. And so it was that at the end of my first year, I became the "Rabbi" of Temple Beth Am of Lindenhurst, Long Island. But before I describe those four wonderful years of a different kind of self- discovery, I need to tell the story of how I participated in a mini-revolution that enabled all that followed to come to pass.

A TRANSFER TO CINCINATI AVERTED

W hen I entered the Jewish Institute of Religion, it was in process of being downsized from a five year to a two year school with students being required to transfer to Cincinnati at the end of their second year. Two classes, the third year and fourth year, had already made that move so that when we began in 1955, in addition to us, only the second year and the fifth year were still in the New York School. This process had begun several years earlier when Rabbi Stephen S. Wise, founder and president of the JIR, found no one to take over its leadership before he died. The word was that he had reached out to Rabbi Mordecai Kaplan whose liberal Reconstructionist Movement was without a seminary of its own, but Kaplan, for whatever reason, refused and remained instead on the faculty of the Conservative Jewish Theological Seminary where he had been a professor for many years. At that point, in 1948, Wise had no choice but to merge his Jewish Institute of Religion with the Hebrew Union College in Cincinnati. Thus, HUC-JIR was born. Its president, Dr. Nelson Glueck, world-renowned archeologist, saw no need for two complete five year programs and after several years proposed that students be given the option of spending their first two years either in New York or Cincinnati, or at the newest campus in Los Angeles. Years three, four and five were to be spent by all in Cincinnati. In addition, he added the possibility of a return to New York for a sixth year, perhaps as a kind of internship to be devoted to practical rabbinics.

Chaim Stern (later to become the editor of the *Gates of Prayer*, the 1975 revision of the classic *Union Prayer Book*), Fred Gottschalk (successor to Nelson Glueck as President of HUC-JIR) and Leonard Kravitz (who was to become a professor at the New York School), were three of the better known students of that era. Among others, they were ordained in Cincinnati instead of at the New York School where they and their classmates had begun their rabbinic studies. We and our second year classmates did not want to go that route. We wanted to stay in New York.

As fortune had it, we had an important ally. Rabbi Louis I. Newman, the prominent rabbi of Congregation Rodeph Shalom in Manhattan and an early graduate of the JIR, was convinced that there had to be a Liberal seminary in New York City, the world's greatest Jewish community outside of Israel. If Nelson Glueck persisted in his attempt to diminish the importance of the New York branch of the HUC-JIR, he would create his own seminary to train Liberal rabbis. He had the support of other New York Reform rabbis and the wherewithal to do just that. Thus the Academy of Jewish Religion (AJR) was born and housed at Rodeph Shalom, some sixteen blocks north of JIR. Several students who had been rejected by HUC-JIR had already started studying there under the tutelage of a rather decent faculty so it was, in fact, a going concern when we started classes at JIR.

While Rabbi Newman promised to shut down the moment JIR reopened full time, he was also, not averse, in the meantime, to soliciting additions to his student body from among those of us who were enrolled at JIR. And so it was that we students in the first and second year classes were courted by the AJR. We would meet with Rabbi Neiman, the administrative head of the AJR who described what we might experience should we decide to switch over. Displaying great *chutzpah*, we would leave a note on the blackboard for our teacher stating that we had gone next door to the SSW Free Synagogue where Rabbi Edward Klein, another disciple of Stephen S. Wise and his successor at the Free Synagogue, welcomed us and gave us a room in which to meet. Rabbi Klein was as upset as Rabbi Newman at what he perceived as an attempt to phase out JIR.

With all that, we were not really anxious to make a change. We had jobs and great opportunities lay in store for us in the years to come. The

Newman School had no official connection to the Reform Movement nor to its placement process. It could provide no guarantee that we would find jobs upon ordination. But at the same time, we did not want to go to HUC in Cincinnati either. Some of my classmates had wives and children for whom a move would have been a great upheaval. Moreover, Cincinnati did not offer the same employment opportunities for its students as did New York with its large cosmopolitan Jewish community. When, as days passed, we attracted support from some members of the Cincinnati student body who indicated that they too were unhappy and would consider making the switch, we suddenly felt we had some power. Not only did we have options, but we did not think Dr. Glueck wanted to lose half of his student body. We indicated as much in a carefully- crafted letter to him in which we stated our desire to stay in New York City at the HUC-JIR but were prepared to transfer to the Newman School if that became impossible.

Our first year passed amidst an air of great uncertainty. We were busy working, both at our studies and at our jobs. One day we would hear that New York was reopening full time and our hopes were raised; the next day, we would hear that it wasn't and we were let down. Our symbol, as suggested by one of our professors who was in a position to receive insider news was the pendulum. It swung this way one day; the school was reopening. It swung back the next; it wasn't. So it went, until May of 1956 when we were summoned to a meet with Dr. Glueck in the Board Room, a space not generally open to students.

At last we would learn our fate. Or so we thought. But after recounting his many difficulties and problems for fifty minutes of the hour, Dr. Glueck had still not addressed what we expected would be the substance of our meeting. Finally, he held up the letter we had sent him much earlier during the school year to which he had never responded and addressed its contents.

Gentlemen: Were I to take your letter seriously, he began, *I would call each of you into my office and ask whether you subscribed to its contents. If you said yes,*

I would shake your hand and wish you well in the future. We held our breaths awaiting the next sentence.

But, he then said, *I do not think you were serious.* At that point we breathed a sigh of relief because we realized we had won. He would not shut down JIR nor would he take action against us. And so the meeting ended and indeed, within a matter of days, word came that the New York School was reopening full time as the New York branch of the Hebrew Union College-Jewish Institute of Religion. Needless to say, we were thrilled. And true to his word, Rabbi Newman ended his relationship to the Academy for Jewish Religion. Several of his students were accepted to HUC-JIR as part of the agreement and became our newest classmates.

But, because it is rare for any Jewish institution to go out of business, the AJR, under the leadership of Rabbi Neiman and with the support of its faculty, found new quarters. It continues as a non-denominational Jewish seminary which trains rabbis and cantors to serve in mainly, but not exclusively, Liberal congregations until this day. Its reputation has improved to the extent that some of the graduates of the Academy for Jewish Religion have, after some years of experience and of proving their competence, been accepted as members of the Central Conference of American Reform Rabbis, the fellowship of Reform rabbis, most of whom are graduates of HUC-JIR. There is, incidentally, also an independent Seminary in California with the same name (AJR) although unconnected to the New York school.

PUTTING LEARNING TO WORK: A STUDENT PULPIT

The back story having been told, we can return to the main narrative. The post-World War II years in and around New York City were times of enormous Jewish growth marked by a move from the inner city to the suburbs. As Jews moved to Long Island, Westchester and New Jersey, they not only built new homes but they established new communities. Having left their inner city synagogues behind, they sought to establish new centers of Jewish life where they could meet like minded new friends, celebrate the Sabbath and Jewish Festivals and provide a Jewish Education for their children. Thus, beginning in the years following WW2 and into the 1950s, there was a marked growth in the creation of new suburban synagogues. Each not only needed teachers for their Religious Schools but, more importantly, rabbis to lead them in prayer, to teach them about Jewish life and to represent their members in the Christian communities in which they now found themselves. Since there were not enough seasoned rabbis to fill all of the pulpits that were seeking spiritual leaders and since the new congregations were usually not in position, at first, to pay full time salaries, they turned to New York's rabbinic seminaries where students were primed to fill those needs. The fact that many of us barely knew more than our congregants did not seem to matter. The need was there and we were more than willing to fill it.

It is against this background that, towards the end of my first year, I was invited to interview for a weekend position at Temple Beth Am, in a southeastern Suffolk County community called Lindenhurst, Long Island, about an hour's drive from where I lived in Laurelton, Queens. The interview consisted of conducting a Sabbath Eve service, preaching a sermon and meeting with the leaders of the forty families who met in small storefront on the main street which was rented for use on Friday evenings. On occasion, anti-Semitic slurs could be heard coming through the screen door which was all that separated us from the sidewalk and the shops next door. Lindenhurst had been a home for the German Bund before World War ll so it came as no surprise. By way of contrast, the Sabbath school and High Holiday services were held in the local Methodist Church which was kind enough to rent the congregation its facilities and whose Pastor, Ralph Morgan, and congregants were most welcoming.

I remember my sermon that night: *Waiting for God*. Samuel Beckett's enigmatic new play *Waiting for Godot* had just made its appearance around that time. While I had not seen it, its title seemed to be an allusion to God, according to some critics. I took off on the idea that it does not serve us well to be passive in waiting for God to do for us. Rather we need to seize hold of our own destiny and to shape the world as God's helpers and co-workers, a conviction that is still very central to my theological belief system. The congregation seemed to have liked what I said for I was asked to become their student rabbi, if not on that very night, than soon after. So began a wonderful four year relationship that saw the congregation double in size and acquire a building of its own (an old church) before I left.

I don't know who benefitted more from that relationship, they or I. I do know that serving as a rabbi in the real world made my studies come to life and presented me with invaluable experience that was to serve me well in later years. It was in Lindenhurst that I developed a preaching and teaching style and where I learned how to handle people in sensitive situations. Most of all, I came to understand that dealing with congregants is an exercise in political savvy as much as it is an exercise in human relations.

The people for the most part came from modest economic backgrounds and lived in very simple homes. They were warm and friendly and apart from an occasional argument over what constituted Reform Judaism, we got along well. I would drive out on Friday afternoon, have dinner with one of the families, conduct Sabbath Eve services and then remain overnight with the same or another family so that on Saturday morning, I was ready for the Religious School which had close to 100 students. I directed a staff of paid teachers most if not all of whom had attended and been certified by the HUC School of Education (described earlier) where I had begun my adult Jewish studies during my college years. Someone played the piano and I led the singing during the weekly assembly. I had only the most basic training in pedagogy (courses in education were part of the seminary curriculum) but my instincts and teaching skills were good and things ran amazingly well. Here I developed a philosophy of Jewish education that sought to combine the acquisition of Jewish knowledge with having a good time. Judging from the feedback, we succeeded pretty well.

One day a parent came to me and asked what it was that I was doing to her children? *What do you mean?* I asked. It seems I had stressed the importance of staying home from school on the Jewish holidays and coming to temple with one's parents, a mantra I was to preach throughout my rabbinate. Accordingly, the child in question had come home and told his parents he wanted to go to services on the holiday in question with the following words: *The Rabbi is like a king. If he says I must go, then I must go.* We both had a good laugh, but indeed, the child and his mother were there the following week. I think that was the height of my power which I could never quite recapture, even with my own children. But it helped make that Lindenhurst experience special.

In addition to conducting Sabbath Eve, *Yom Tov* and High Holiday services, serving as principal of the Religious School and officiating at an occasional funeral (funerals were OK but by NY State law, I was not licensed to officiate at weddings prior to ordination) I did all the things a rabbi was expected to do, even if in a very part time way and even though I was years away from having earned that title. I visited the sick, did some counseling when that was needed, attended an occasional meeting when my presence was requested and represented the congregation in the community, whether to give an invocation at a graduation, to speak to the local Lions Club or to meet with the local clergy.

I also taught the Confirmation class. Gerry Rivera, who later changed his name to Geraldo and became a prominent TV personality, was my student. He mentioned me in one of his books claiming that I, a gentle young rabbi, officiated at his Bar Mitzvah. In fact it was not his Bar Mitzvah. Rather it was his Confirmation, together with his older sister Irene and several other students.

All the while I was learning on the job. But on Saturday afternoon, when my work was done, I drove back home and got ready for the new week, usually satisfied with what I had accomplished and enriched by the experience. For that I was paid $2,500 per year at first which eventually became $3500 by my fourth year; not a vast sum but enough to enable me to cover some of my expenses and have a little left over.

As the years went on and as the membership grew to eighty families, it was evident that there was need for a more permanent place to carry out its program and to establish its own identity. The Methodist Church was most cooperative in allowing us to remove crosses each Saturday morning and on the High Holidays and to put a sheet over the Christmas tree in December, but it was time to have a place of our own. And while the congregation had limited means, the search for a building eventually led to the purchase of an old abandoned Lutheran Church. Though I was not to reap the reward, we did move in and held a service in that building a few weeks before I came to the end of my tenure at Temple Beth Am. I consider that something of a major accomplishment. Unfortunately, the great hopes that had built up over the years never materialized after I left even though I was succeeded by an ordained rabbi. Not long thereafter, Temple Beth Am closed its doors and the congregants joined another Reform congregation in the general proximity. I have often wondered what might have happened had I been able to remain for a few more years.

What I do not have to wonder about is how kind and accepting the members were to me and, especially during the last two years, to Brenda, the woman who was to become my wife in June of 1959, as I entered my final year of rabbinic studies. They embraced her as they had embraced me, gave her a lovely bridal shower and gave us wedding gifts some of which we still use to this very day. For many years we maintained contact with several of the families from those long ago days when we were young and filled with dreams of tomorrow. They were an important part of my spiritual journey which now became our journey, for Brenda would share it with me.

NO LONGER ALONE

We met in August of 1958. I was still living at home notwithstanding that I was only months from turning twenty-five, *the age of reduced automobile insurance*, as we called it. I had once proposed taking my own apartment in the city with my friend Stanley, but my Jewish mother laid her usual guilt trip on me by asking me whether I didn't love her for why else would I want to move away when I didn't have to? Being a caring and obedient son and not wanting to cause my mother any distress, I quickly withdrew my question and remained at home, leaving Stanley to room with another friend. But, one could say with the sages, *gam zu le tovah (this too was for the best),* for had I lived in the city I would not have been in front of my house walking my dog when Phyllis Goldberg drove up in her parent's flashy yellow Cadillac with a certain Brenda Anne Schiffman sitting next to her in the front seat. I knew Phyllis through her sister Marion who had been my car-pool ride to Queens College during that earlier time when I didn't own a car. She was looking for my friend Steve who lived directly across the street from me and whom she was pursuing. (She was successful and I eventually co-officiated at their wedding). Brenda, her closest friend, from the time when both girls were in the Brownies to this day, was along for the ride. As Phyllis rolled down the window, I walked over and was introduced as *Ralph the Rabbi*. While I could not see too well in the dark, it did seem to me that this young woman was rather cute - tall and thin with short hair. We chatted for a few minutes but then went our separate ways, the car driving off and I continuing, to walk my dog Terri.

The following weekend, however, we were all invited to a party in Greenwich Village, known as a Bohemian area in lower Manhattan. I needed a date as did Brenda. Phyllis was the matchmaker. She asked

Brenda whether she preferred going with *Ralph the Rabbi,* whom she had just met, or *Lee the Medical Student* who had just returned from a trip to Europe. Being well brought up with proper Jewish values, Brenda naturally chose the budding doctor over the aspiring rabbi who therefore was matched up with another friend, Alice. The party was great except for the fact that Brenda found her date to be *full of himself,* as she would later put it, and I was more than a little annoyed that my date kept calling me Frank - a lovely name, but not mine. So at some point during the evening, Brenda and I left our designated dates and drifted towards each other, beginning a relationship that culminated in our engagement the following February and marriage on Brenda's twenty-first birthday, June 21, 1959, which as it happens was also Father's Day.

Brenda's parents were both New York City school teachers. Her mother Elsie whom I sadly never met died tragically of cancer when Brenda was but fourteen leaving her father David, a marvelous man, to be both father and mother to her and to her younger brother Henry. David taught at Andrew Jackson High School in Queens and later became science chairman at Bushwick High School in Brooklyn. He supplemented his income by teaching religious school at Central Synagogue of Rockville Center where he was a beloved faculty member. When it came time for the wedding, it was natural that we should go there - a decision we never regretted.

My mentor, Herbert Baumgard, by this time living in Miami, was able to stop on his way to a Reform Rabbi's Convention and officiated at our ceremony. Because wine is one of the symbols used during the Jewish wedding, he used the image of the grapevine to remind us to direct our reach and our vision upwards but also to make sure that we were firmly planted in the ground of reality. He understood all too well that rabbis sometimes tend to have their heads in the clouds and forget about what goes on in the real world. I must confess to using that image myself, with variations, on more than one occasion during weddings I performed in the early years of my rabbinate. I also have tried to live by that principle in my actions and in my preaching. Indeed, for me, to be a Jew is always to live in two worlds: the world of dreams and visions of a world which might be; and the world as it really is. Our goal is to bring the two together; to transform one into the other.

During the first year of our married life, we moved into a small apartment in Briarwood, Queens. It had only one room and a closet-sized kitchen. It also had a small closed-in space off the bedroom/living room (we had a sofa bed) just large enough to fit a desk and a chair. It was there that I worked on my thesis during that fifth year of rabbinical school and there that Brenda eventually typed it. I often joke that I married her because I needed someone to type my thesis.

In the meantime, she had also graduated from Queens College and found placement as a teacher in a small wooden schoolhouse (one of only a few that remained in the city) not far from where we lived. She taught a group of third graders all of whom were African-American. I, now in my fifth year at HUC-JIR, attended classes and on weekends, served my Lindenhurst congregation, which became more special because Brenda came with me. From the beginning, Brenda was a wonderful rabbi's wife sharing the joys and sorrows of the rabbinate and of our congregants with me. In fact, before I proposed, I questioned her as to how she felt about becoming a *rebbetzin*; whether she would be willing to attend services regularly with me, be present at Sisterhood meetings and at congregational events and, in general, be part of that aspect of my life. Before we were even formally engaged, I asked her to stop working at Lord and Taylor where she had a Saturday job. *How will it look if the rabbi's wife violates the Sabbath?* I asked. Stop she did though she continued to enjoy shopping there even without the employee discount.

And so our partnership was forged and while I do not pretend to speak for Brenda, I believe it to have been a wonderful partnership that has, as of this writing, extended for well over fifty years. I must admit that while I think I understand the new world of feminism, women's equality and *Leaning In* as my most famous Bat Mitzvah, Sheryl Sandberg put it, I find it difficult to comprehend how a marriage can succeed when one partner does not share a passion for the work of the other. I feel bad for those of my colleagues whose spouses live separate lives and are not an integral part of the congregational life, which is at times as all-consuming as it is enriching. I say this not because I wish to engage in a discussion on what makes a good marriage but in order to say that I cannot imagine my personal spiritual journey to have been anywhere near as meaningful had not my wife regularly sat before me at services, at first alone and later with our children; or stood by my side in the synagogue greeting people and reminding me of names or facts I might have forgotten. It was she who made sure the Sabbath table was set every Friday night, that we had the appropriate holiday foods in their seasons and that we got to temple on time. And it was she who was understanding when congregational activities robbed her and our children of precious family time together. To be sure, we live in a different era. There are many two career families today which do not allow for the luxury of a *stay-at-home mom* in the manner we lived. But still, if a rabbi's family cannot be united in matters of Jewish life, than I worry about the future of the Jewish people.

The year between 1959 and 1960 was filled with activity. Not only were we getting used to the life of a young married couple, but my duties in Lindenhurst together with course work and the writing of my thesis did not allow for too much leisure time activity. Nevertheless we did maintain a somewhat active social life with our friends and spent a bit of time wondering where the next year would take us which, as it turned out, was to Clark Air Base in the Philippines. Little did I think that my spiritual journey would take me to such a far-away place, but when Uncle Sam issues an invitation, it is hard to turn it down.

THE AIR FORCE BECKONS

When I became a pre-rabbinic student, I was given a deferment from the draft with the understanding that upon completion of my seminary studies, I would, if needed, *volunteer* to serve a term as a military chaplain. It was the period after the Korean War and before the start of our serious involvement in Vietnam but the draft was still in effect. All three branches of the service had Jews who required and deserved spiritual guidance. So I, along with seven other ordainees from HUC-JIR and a like number from the JTS and Yeshiva University were chosen to serve as military chaplains for two or three years depending on their branch of service and their assignments. In order to determine who among us from HUC-JIR was to go, the students on both the New York and Cincinnati campuses had drawn up eligibility lists which began with single graduates at the top of the list followed by those who were married but were as yet without children. Those who were married with children were last in line. It was the Jewish Welfare Board as the certifying and coordinating agency which made the final determination albeit only after it was learned whether or not we passed the military's physical.

Not until late in the school year, after I had interviewed for and been invited to accept an assistantship in Glencoe, Illinois, did I receive a letter from the United States government ordering me to report to Chaplain School at Lackland Air Force Base in San Antonio, Texas for a six- week stay. Thereafter, I was to proceed to Travis Air Force Base outside of San Francisco from which I was to fly to Clark Air Force Base in the Philippines where I was to serve for two years as 13th AF Jewish Chaplain. We had been allowed to choose our branch of service and I had chosen the Air Force. I felt that the selection of bases was more appealing and would allow me to bring Brenda as a dependent. Some Army and Navy tours would not have allowed me that privilege, and I wanted to minimize the risk of being separated from my new bride. But the Philippines was surely not on my radar. Nor did I realize that its location was some 13,000 miles from New York thinking it was near Hawaii. I misguidedly looked forward to weekends in Honolulu. Despite my brilliant sense of geography, it turned out to be a wonderful experience in a part of the world that I would not have otherwise experienced for a long time, if ever. Not only that, but I had the opportunity to serve my country in a most meaningful way.

On June 6, 1960 I was ordained as a rabbi with my classmates by Dr. Nelson Glueck in a very impressive service at New York's majestic Temple Emanuel. Had the Air Force not beckoned, I might have gone to Glencoe or even perhaps stayed in Lindenhurst for several more years and tried to make it into a more viable congregation for they were serious about going beyond the student rabbi status. But it was not to be. Instead we said our goodbyes at Temple Beth Am, which gave Brenda and me a loving sendoff, and prepared to start on a brand new adventure – The United States Air Force – where we were to discover an entirely new way of life.

The first stop in this next leg of my spiritual journey would take Brenda and me across the United States to Lackland Air Force Base, a large Air Force training base in San Antonio, Texas. There I attended six weeks of chaplain school together with three other Reform colleagues, several Orthodox and Conservative rabbis as well as an assortment of Protestant and Catholic clergymen. The Christian clergy were planning to make the Air Force their career while we Jews, for the most part, were there to fulfill our obligations and to return to civilian life as soon as possible. As it happened, one of our Jewish colleagues had a change of heart along the way and became a career chaplain. But he was an exception.

None of us, of course, had a clue about military etiquette, the chain of command or even how to march in a parade or salute; not to speak of what we were supposed to do once we arrived at our assigned tour of duty. But that was why we were in chaplain school. So after we were fitted for our uniforms (dress and casual) at the mainly Jewish-owned stores that specialized in such matters, we reported for duty and began our course of study. Our training, even as it introduced us to a world which was very foreign to most of us rabbis who had grown up in much more parochial environments, turned out to be quite pleasant. When it ended, we were set to proceed to our assignments. If not fully versed in what we were supposed to do, we had at least become somewhat familiar with the new culture of which we were now a part.

The experience of mingling with clergymen who came from different faith systems was both eye-opening and also extremely valuable. Not only did we learn about *them* but *they* learned about us. We came to understand how we had to function in a world which was overwhelmingly not Jewish and far-removed from the Jewish cocoons in which we tended to spin our lives. As a result, when we returned to civilian life at the end of our tours of duty we were better able to deal with non-Jewish clergy in matters of community interest then we had been before.

To a certain extent, it also held true of our relationships to our Orthodox colleagues for many of whom, this was their first time away from familiar surroundings. They were not likely to have had much contact with Reform Jews, certainly not during their Yeshiva days and even less with non-Jews. But the beautiful part of the experience in chaplain school was that we all got along together marvelously well, respectful of differences while having a sense of common cause. Would that we could replicate such an environment in the real world in which we all live. Alas, in many large communities, Orthodox rabbis will not sit at the same table with non-Orthodox rabbis. How sad! In later years, the inability to bring the traditionalists and liberals together in the context of our rabbinic association would be one of the great disappointments of my life.

At the end of six weeks, sometime in mid-September, we graduated and made our way to our various destinations as per the official orders each of us had received. Brenda and I got into our 1958 Chevrolet, waved goodbye to the little apartment we had occupied during chaplain school and began what seemed like an endless drive out of Texas to get to California where I was to report to Travis Air Force Base to begin my long journey to Clark Air Base. In fairness, we did stop for a little *R and R* at Las Vegas along the way as well as in the Los Angeles and San Francisco areas where we visited with relatives. Since our trip ran into the High Holidays, we stopped at Reform congregations en route and were made to feel very much at home: Rosh Hashanah in Bakersfield, CA and Yom Kippur in Palo Alto where the rabbi invited me to read a bit of the service on Yom Kippur afternoon.

But then, the fun ended. After a little more than a year of marriage, Brenda and I bid each other a tearful farewell. She returned east to her parents where she was to await orders before she could fly to join me; I flew west into the sunset to my assignment as 13th Air Force Chaplain. It was our first separation, and I did not like the feeling. This was one of the reasons I did not remain in the military at the end of my two years even though there were many advantages to making the military one's career, especially as an officer. I was to discover later, in counseling situations, that separations were actually good for some military marriages which seemed to flourish better when the spouses were apart thus validating the old cliché that *absence makes the heart grow fonder*. But not for me! Fortunately, our separation was of brief duration. Given the waiting list for on base housing, I found off-base housing nearby in a town called Angeles soon after I arrived. Brenda was able to join me in less than two months.

I boarded my flight to the Philippine Islands on the eve of Sukkot to begin the forty-hour journey, something I would never do today since I avoid travelling on the Sabbath and Jewish holidays. But then, I knew no better. Orders were orders! So off I went on an old-fashioned, four engine, propeller plane courtesy of MATS (the Military Air Transport Command), which made three stops - Honolulu, Wake Island and Guam - before finally landing at Clark Air Base where I reported for duty as Chaplain Lieutenant Ralph P. Kingsley. Somewhere along the way, during the seemingly endless flight, we crossed the International Date

Line, skipping a day while moving forward on the calendar. That was the year I lost *Sukkot*.

It was rainy and extremely humid when I got off the plane at Clark Air Base, about sixty miles north of Manila. The rainy season begins there during the summer and continues well into the fall. It is also a time for hurricanes but we were lucky to have been spared during our time at Clark. As a New Yorker, I was, of course, not used to such weather patterns. But with the passing of the months, we actually grew fond of the climate - the sunshine, the warmth and the lack of snow and cold winters - which is part of the reason we chose to settle in Miami seven years later. But that gets ahead of the story.

I spent the weeks before Brenda's arrival living in the bachelor officer's quarters, meeting the Jewish community on base, relating to my superiors and getting used to the military way of life, especially the chain of command to which I was still not quite accustomed. I was used to thinking for myself, making my own decisions and coming and going as I pleased. This is not the way of the military where one is subject to the command of the person who is superior in rank and thus has control over one's actions. That took a little getting used to. Interestingly, Herman Woulk, in his classic novel *The Caine Mutiny*, defends that system for, in a way, it mirrors the Jewish Orthodoxy to which he was committed. God is the ultimate *Commander*, as it were, whose command is to be followed and not to be questioned even when, as in the case of Captain Queeg, it does not seem rational.

In contrast, it is not difficult to understand why we in the liberal religious camp might find such an authoritarian approach difficult, and in a larger sense, why there are relatively few Jews who choose the military as a career. We tend to be a questioning people who need to be given reasons for what we are told to do and more often than not, are apt to challenge authority. Still, as in any orthodoxy, once one accepts the rules, the system works well and attracts a certain population who choose the military as a career. The very structure that may be problematic for some can be very satisfying for others, providing security and certainty.

As far as I know, only the Israeli Army successfully allows for a degree of informality in its structure. But then, why should we be surprised? Isn't that typical of us Jews?

Philosophical issues aside, I was quickly taken under wing by some of the more seasoned career military who were stationed at Clark and made to feel at home. But most of my new congregants were dental and medical officers who were counting the days till they could fulfill their obligation to Uncle Sam and return home. In addition, there were the enlisted personnel, some attached to the Air Force and others attached to the Army, most of whom were serving out their enlistment or draft obligations but some of whom had also chosen the military as their career. The nice thing was that they could all come together in the context of the Jewish chaplain's program. Regardless of rank, as members of the Jewish people, a unique family, they stood as equals before God.

My main responsibilities were predictable: conducting services, running a Jewish education program for adults and for children of military personnel, counseling, visiting with the troops during and after working hours, seeing to it that there were sufficient supplies for Jewish holidays such as *matzot* on *Pesach* and, in general, making sure that there was as much normal Jewish life as was possible given our location thousands of miles away from home. I also had occasion to officiate at two weddings of which one was the only marriage I ever performed in which one of the parties was not Jewish. I was not aware of that fact until it was too late to make other arrangements. But the bride studied with me for a year after the wedding and converted. She and her husband both subsequently became observant and now live in Israel. I am still in touch with them, just as I am in touch with a, then, young man at whose Bar Mitzvah I presided. He is today functioning as a rabbi in a neighboring community and gives me credit for his career choice. Just two of many heart-warming stories that all of us who served as chaplains can recount.

But there was also a major PR component. I, as the Jewish Chaplain, was the official personification of the Jew in a world that was largely Gentile. When I interacted with non-Jews, whether in a military or a social environment, I not only represented myself in my military persona but I also was seen as the embodiment of Jewish life. For some of the airmen and even officers, I was the first Jew they had ever met, something difficult for people like me who grew up in a largely Jewish environment to understand. I viewed it as one of my responsibilities to sensitize the non-Jews to Jewish values and concerns; for example, especially at times like Christmas when Christian symbolism made our Jewish minority status especially apparent causing some degree of discomfort. Trying to point to the *wall of the separation of church and state,* for example, made for some interesting discussions. Even though they did not decrease the presence of Christian symbolism during those holiday times, and sometimes placed me in an uncomfortable adversarial position with the overwhelmingly Christian population on base, they led to what I hope was a much better understanding of the mind and heart of the Jew.

While I have actively defended that *wall of separation* throughout the years of my rabbinate, I have also become less of a purist, understanding the need to live in the real world and, at times, needing to make accommodations for the sake of a greater good even at the cost of an absolute principle. In retrospect, I would probably approach those holiday times in a less confrontational way today and seek more positive ways to defend and elevate the minority status of my people.

Although my major focus was at Clark Air Base, a TAC (Tactical Air Command) facility, I was also responsible for visiting Naval and Marine personnel at Sangley Naval Station in Manila, Subic Naval Station and Cubi Point Naval Air Station. The latter two were both on the island of Luzon several hours by car from Clark. In addition, once each month, I boarded a military flight to Taiwan where I served Air Force and Army personnel stationed in Taipei and Tainan. Several times during my tour of duty, I flew to Saigon and Bangkok to visit with Jewish Americans stationed there who were either in the military or attached to the United States Embassy in a civilian capacity. These were the days immediately before the Vietnam War so all was relatively peaceful. But the Viet Cong had started their guerilla attacks and one could sense that future days would be less tranquil. In Vietnam, I had my only real military experience, sleeping in a tent protected by a mosquito net in the city of Denang on what was to be the dangerous Vietcong infested Route One. While the TDY (temporary duty) travel experiences were interesting, highlighted by a brief time spent in Saigon, a beautiful city with wide boulevards and stunning women, and in the exotic Bangkok with its dirty canals and expansive Buddhist temples, I was always happy to get back to Clark and Brenda unscathed.

Among the benefits of being stationed sixty miles north of Manila was the fact that Brenda and I automatically were welcomed into the Manila Jewish community which numbered perhaps one hundred twenty or so families. Some of them were German Jews who had fled from Hitler but because they were Germans were treated fairly well during the days of the Japanese occupation. The Japanese had no particular animus against Jews so treated them as they did other Germans. Others had come from Shanghai to which they had fled from Russia or Iraq and then to the Philippines. Still others were Americans; former GIs who remained after the war to make a new life for themselves in very promising economic conditions or business people, more recently arrived, looking to tap new markets. Some were even native born Filipinos who had married into Jewish families with or without benefit of conversion.

And, of course, there were a few who had Israel connections. There was an Israeli Consul, Yehiel Ilsar, who was elevated to the rank of ambassador soon after Golda Meir made a state visit in 1961. Brenda and I sat next to her at a special dinner given in her honor by the members of Temple Emil, a congregation rebuilt after the war with the help of American soldiers and Jewish money. What a thrill that was. She was a most unattractive woman, physically, but her ability to communicate verbally was extraordinary. I still remember the theme of her spellbinding remarks that night, which took place on *Tu B'shvat,* the New Year of the Trees. She spoke of how in the midst of winter, surrounded by mounds of snow, Russian Jewish children would celebrate because it was tree planting time in Israel and of how, wherever Jews live and whatever the season of the year, they are connected to the land of Israel and the rhythm of its calendar. It was a message that has become part of my very being.

Altogether, Manila's Jews were a most interesting and welcoming group. Whenever possible, Brenda and I would visit Manila and on a number of occasions, I was invited to speak at the Sabbath morning service and even to officiate when one of their young people became a Bar Mitzvah. It was there that I learned a lesson from a wise elderly gentleman, Mr. Levine, who was a past president of the congregation and had lived through a great deal without ever losing his faith. When I commented on how well the young *Bar Mitzvah* boy was prepared, he sagely said: *A parrot too can learn a Haftarah,* which was to say, there is more to being a Jew then learning to chant Hebrew by rote. In later years, I had many occasions to quote those words to children and parents in my classes.

As I reflect back on those two years, I regret that I did not make better use of them. While we went to Japan and Hong Kong, both of which were amazing places, in addition to the areas my duties took me, we could have done much more travelling in South East Asia at no cost to ourselves (Space available military travel is free). And we could have taken up Temple Emil on its offer for me to become its rabbi and lived handsomely on the Philippine economy for a few years, paid in United States dollars. Instead, we saved my leave time (thirty days per year) so we could return to the states more quickly to return to civilian life there. George Bernard Shaw was right. Youth is indeed wasted on the young.

That notwithstanding, those two years were very special, not only in terms of people we met and places we visited but in learning that there was much more to life and to the world than the small area of Long Island in which we both grew up. Ever since those days, Brenda and I have both enjoyed travelling to new places and meeting new people in this extraordinary world in which we live. And amazingly, even after the loss of one third of our population during the Holocaust, wherever one goes in the world, there are Jews. And wherever there are Jews, the community in which they live is the better for it. I only wish there would be more time and that we had more resources to go to all of the places we still haven't been.

Though both Brenda and I were anxious to return to our families and to move forward with our lives, two years in the Far East were, in retrospect, years of growth and discovery. This was my first true encounter with the real world of non-Jews. We were a distinct minority and yet, as Jewish Chaplain I was treated with great respect and was privy, with my top secret clearance, to much more information than the average officer. While I represented a very small minority, in terms of the number of Jews in the military or even in the United States, I was treated as if I represented fully a third of the religious spectrum of *Catholic, Protestant and Jew* as the writer Will Herberg had pointed out in his classic 1950's book. It was for me an important lesson about the place of the Jew in this great American society where we have had access, to reiterate the writer Max Lerner's term, in ways not experienced by Jews in any earlier period of our history or in any other country in the world. We should never take that for granted.

COMING HOME

Jet service, which was still quite new in 1962, was about to be instituted as our tour drew to a close. Had we waited another week and not been so impatient, we could have taken advantage of it and avoided the forty hour flight to the west coast. But getting home a week or two sooner was more important to us at the time than our comfort. As things happened, it was a good choice for it expedited the next leg of my spiritual journey, a stop at the Garden City Jewish Center which was most anxious to find a new spiritual leader in time for the fast approaching High Holidays. I had submitted an application to their pulpit search committee and while they indicated that they would wait, I was concerned lest they engage another candidate before our return.

And so we boarded a propeller plane at the earliest opportunity for the flight back to the United States where I was to be discharged, but not in the same way we had left. We were culturally enriched, both by our contact with the indigenous population of the Philippines and the aura of South East Asia and the Far East which we came to know in our several trips to Japan and Hong Kong, among other points of interest. But, more than that, largely as a result of our military experience, our intellectual and social horizons were greatly extended beyond our somewhat parochial upbringings. And best of all, we brought a special package home with us, a newborn son just six weeks old when we took off for San Francisco on the long trip home.

Evan Moses had been born at the Clark Air Base Hospital. He arrived a month late, much to everyone's consternation, but quickly became our most prized addition. The obstetrician, a career officer, asked whether I wanted to be present for the birth but I declined and paced the waiting area for what seemed an eternity until at long last, I heard cries coming from the delivery room followed by the appearance of a doctor friend who had assisted with the delivery. *Is he all there; ten fingers, ten toes..?* I asked. On being told that everything was perfect, I spoke the words of the *Shehecheyanu*, thanking the Eternal for having kept me alive and bringing me to that incredible moment in my life and that of my BBB (beautiful beloved Brenda) who had done all of the labor while I just *kvelled* with pride.

I cannot begin to describe the joy of that moment. It was only to be matched when eight days later, we brought our new born son into the Covenant of Abraham, one of the two most meaningful spiritual experiences of my life – the other having been the circumcision of our second son, Jonathan. We invited the entire Jewish Military Community and our new friends from Temple Emil in Manila to the event which took place in our on-base house to which we had been assigned after about a year of living off-base. There was a lavish spread provided by the Officer's Club (whose commander was Jewish), replete with *challah* loaves and chopped liver for all of which we paid $35 (You can't beat military prices). But for me the day was all about the ceremony itself, the enactment of a ritual that can be traced back to the very beginnings of Jewish life and links us and our children to all the generations who have come before us; back to the very first Jew, *Avraham Aveenu*, who gave the world the notion that there was a transcending, unifying force in the world – a *Power not ourselves* we call God.

There was no *mohel* in the area, but there was a Jewish Air Force Pediatrician who was thrilled to be asked to preside, although I was to recite the appropriate prayers. Unlike *mohalim*, doctors frequently use a certain clamp to restrict the flow of blood which requires a waiting period before the actual cut is made. During that period, quite spontaneously, I asked whether I might do the cut myself since the *Mitzvah* of Circumcision is incumbent upon the father. Dr. Pakula, himself a sensitive Jew, was only too happy to accommodate me. And so, when the right amount of time had passed, he handed me the scalpel and guided my hand as I actually got to circumcise my son. What an extraordinary spiritual experience!

When our second son, Jonathan Meir was born four-and-a-half years later, I naturally wanted to replicate the experience. This time it was a *mohel* who presided and set things up, albeit not with a clamp but with a special shield called a *Magen* which protects the glans of the penis from harm while allowing the easy removal of the foreskin. That second experience equaled the first in its emotional impact. Whatever health benefits that circumcision might provide (and despite occasional challenges by fringe elements, the overwhelming evidence, time after time is that benefits far outweigh any perceived harm), for me the value of circumcision is clearly in its historical and spiritual aspect which binds parent to child and our people to its proud history in a most special way that can only be understood by those who have experienced it.

We were a bit concerned about travelling home with an infant barely six weeks old but he withstood the trip beautifully, aided by some attentive stewardesses who kept us well supplied with warm milk to supplement that which Brenda supplied naturally from her nursing breasts. Forty hours or so after take- off, after the same stops we made on the way west, and having recaptured the day we lost crossing the International Date Line, we landed on United States soil at Travis Air Force Base, accomplished the several day process of being discharged and flew the last leg back to New York. There we were reunited with our parents from whom we had been separated for two years. While they were delighted to see us, they were even more delighted finally to meet and hold their new grandson for the first time.

We temporarily moved in with Brenda's father, my biggest fan whom I always called Dad and with his second wife Dorothy, a colleague at Bushwick High School where he was science chairman and she taught Latin. David had married her while Brenda and I were on our honeymoon, and they were to live happily together for more than forty years. Needless to say, he was delighted and thrilled to have immediate access to his first grandchild whose English name, Evan, was after Brenda's mother Elsie who had died when Brenda was fourteen, creating thereby a special bond. The side benefit, of course, apart from our not having to pay rent, was that we had built-in baby-sitters.

It did not take us very long to readjust to civilian life though I remember being somewhat (happily) surprised when I learned that one teller in the bank could handle both deposits and withdrawals and that you didn't have to stand on separate lines as in the military where everything was compartmentalized. Nor did I have to account for every moment of my time to a higher ranking person. My life was again my own. The military has many advantages, at least in peacetime, but independent thought and action are not among them.

MY FIRST REAL CONGREGATION

Within a day of returning I called the pulpit chairman at the Garden City Jewish Center and arranged for an interview. I could tell from the phone conversation that they were as excited about meeting me as I was about meeting them. Sure enough, within a matter of days, the initial interview with the selection committee took place. I had been prepped by several of the leaders of the congregation who had determined that I was the right person for them which made the interviewing process much easier. Shortly thereafter, I was introduced to the Congregation at a larger meeting and elected as Rabbi of the Garden City Jewish Center, a position I held for four-and-a- half fulfilling years.

The GCJC was a special place. It was only five or so years old when I arrived. Its first (student) rabbi was a classmate of mine but my immediate predecessor was a much older man who had come out of retirement to serve for several years. At its founding, the congregation had to endure a legal battle, fueled, some say, by anti-Semitism because Garden City was a restricted community where Jews were not welcome. Indeed, to this very day, that mystique has kept Jews from settling there in any significant number despite the fact that it is a lovely community with an outstanding school system. As is often the case, the official reason for the denial of the necessary zoning variance was that the community claimed not to want a House of Worship in the midst of a residential neighborhood. But thanks to a non-Jewish attorney by the name of C. Walter Randall, who based his brief on the precedent of a similar case in another Long Island community, the GCJC was permitted to proceed with its purchase of the former Wrigley Estate, a large home on the corner of Nassau Blvd. and Newmarket St. which it converted into use as a synagogue. Several of the downstairs rooms became the sanctuary and the upstairs bedrooms were used to house the small but growing religious school. There was a large space for a rabbi's study on the second floor and a live-in caretaker had an apartment on the third floor. Fortuitously, there was even an old built-in pipe organ in the area used for the sanctuary, which must have once been a music room. Some years after my arrival, we had it restored to its former glory.

While at first, the imaginative use of space accommodated the needs of the congregation, with time and as the congregation grew, it became evident that we needed to expand. So in 1965, we built an addition to the building which gave us a meeting hall with a kitchen, an administrative office and a brand new rabbi's study, smaller than the room upstairs but much more strategically located. It perfectly suited our needs. This was the first experience I had with a synagogue building program. Many more would follow in future years.

One of the earliest questions that faced the GCJC, even before my time, was whether the congregation was to become Reform or Conservative. By the narrowest of margins, the advocates for Reform won out, probably because the Union of American Hebrew Congregations had a much better sales program than the Conservative United Synagogue of America. But also because it allowed for more choices even as it had fewer restrictions. That is, one could be a Reform Jew and reject or affirm elements of the tradition (*kippot*, a Kosher Kitchen, two days of *Yom Tov* etc.) whereas if one chose to affiliate with the Conservative movement, one was bound by adherence to Jewish Law (*halacha*) in a much more restrictive way.

Having cast its lot with the Reform movement, the traditions of the GCJC nevertheless sought to bridge the narrow divide that resulted in its becoming a Reform congregation. Publically, it encouraged the wearing of *kippot* and *talitot* as well as the observance of two days of Rosh Hashanah from its very beginnings and did not veer away from that practice even as, privately, its members practiced their Judaism in a wide variety of ways. While I had grown up in a classical Reform environment, I had become more observant as the years passed and was very comfortable being in a congregation that was somewhat traditional. Both what I had learned at Temple Bnai Israel in Elmont under the tutelage of its Rabbi, my mentor Herbert Baumgard, and then, my experience in the military where I, as a Reform rabbi, had nonetheless to serve the needs of a broad spectrum of Jews, many of whom were not Reform, made my coming to Garden City a most natural occurrence.

I had come to believe that being a Liberal or Reform Jew was not so much a matter of what one did or did not do as much as it was an approach to why and how one did it. Thus, one could, in theory, as Rabbi Dr. Solomon Freehoff, to whom I referred earlier, once suggested, be Orthodox in practice (orthopraxis) while still being philosophically a Reform Jew. The differentiating feature was that for the Orthodox Jew, Jewish practice came about because Jewish Law, as revealed by God and interpreted by the Rabbis, demanded it be carried out in a certain way. There was a coercive dimension involved. For the Liberal Jew, it came to pass as a result of personal choice, although that choice needed to be informed by the tradition from which it emerged.

While I could not by any stretch of the imagination have been mistaken for being Orthodox, I began to understand, as a result of my studies and my experience, that choice could lead one as easily to affirm the tradition as to reject it even if for reasons totally different than those of the Orthodox Jew. Unfortunately, the Reform Judaism of the early days was identified, for some very understandable reasons, mainly with rejection, as in *Reform Jews do not keep Kosher and pray without hats…*I and a new generation of liberal-thinking Jews was beginning to discover that one could reclaim some of what had been rejected while still functioning within the Liberal or Reform camp. It was a matter of allowing the tradition to have a call on one's life and to take it more seriously than I had in the past, as I sought to give expression to Jewish values and beliefs.

The tradition, having two thousand and more years going for it, deserved to be taken seriously, at least as a first step, and not to be dismissed out of hand as was commonplace among the early Reformers. If an observance resonated with earlier generations, even though it had fallen into disuse, perhaps there was meaning to be found once again by a new generation of Jews who wanted to connect to their people and their God. So why not encourage a return to some once forgotten practices so long as they withstood the test of reasonableness as, for example *Selichot* prayers and *Tashlich* (customs associated with *Rosh HaShanah*) or even observance of the Dietary Laws, fully or in some modified form? On the other hand, observances that were grounded in superstition or in violation of western standards of rationality or credulity such as believing that by swinging a dead chicken over one's head one could get rid of ones sins (*shlaggen kepores*) or asserting that the dead will arise out of their graves on the final Judgment Day and come back to life, are clearly beyond the pale and ought to remain as no more than historical curiosities.

In determining a process by which to fashion a meaningful and positive Jewish way of living that would bring together elements of the tradition with the best of modern thought while providing a way to frame my teaching, another great Jewish thinker offered a rationale: Rabbi Mordecai Kaplan. He had begun his career as an Orthodox rabbi but at a certain point, parted ways with his congregation, The Jewish Center of Manhattan, and founded a new synagogue down the street which he called The Society for the Advancement of Judaism or SAJ. It would become the laboratory for his ideas and programs and the center of the movement he founded, Reconstructionism, the fourth stream of Jewish life today. He was, in my view, the most influential Jewish thinker of the twentieth century even though he is not given nearly the credit he so rightly deserves.

On a programmatic level, he envisioned the synagogue as being not only a praying place and a place of learning but, literally, a center of Jewish communal activity where Jews could come together to give expression to their Jewishness in a variety of ways. From there it was only a short step to the creation of what has become the largely secular institution called the Jewish Community Center or JCC which, together with the synagogue, is central to Jewish life today and for which Kaplan deserves the credit. Over the course of years, many synagogues, mainly though not exclusively in the Conservative movement tried to fulfill that goal in their own way, my new congregation being not the least among them.

On a theological level, Kaplan, like the early and present day Reformers, rejected the basis of Orthodoxy, namely the Divine revelation of scripture and the belief that all of Jewish practice was God given. But he was critical of Reform Judaism for its earlier disavowal of Jewish peoplehood and its anti- Zionist stance. As an advocate of what became known as *Religious Naturalism* because he eschewed the supernatural, he understood the inherent conflict between religion and science that came from seeing Judaism as the revealed word of God. But he also argued that one needed to view Judaism as being more than *only* the religion of the Jewish People, which is how the classical reformers had viewed it. He called it instead, the *Civilization of the Jewish People* which, was not revealed but had rather evolved historically and sociologically over the centuries. While what is generally called religion may have been the central core of the civilization, he believed that there was more to being Jewish than belief in God, prayer and the ethical system derived therefrom.

After all, we share a common history, language (actually two: Hebrew and Yiddish), attachment to a land- Israel- our own art, music and literature as well ceremonies that mark the Jewish calendar and sanctify the events of our cycle of life. These are all features of a civilization. Our sacred books (Torah and Talmud), the Sabbath and Festivals and customs such as the laws of *Kashrut,* are what Kaplan called the *sancta* of our civilization, the sacred times, events and practices that bind Jews together.

In like manner, Americans are united by common language, land, history, Constitution, and national holidays, many of them marking events in American history, for example Memorial Day, July 4th and Thanksgiving. It is through its *sancta* that the values that drive a civilization emerge.

Thus the Jew has lived in two civilizations wherever his wanderings took him. What has been so fortuitous about our life in America and what has made America so hospitable to Jews is that the values that inhere in both civilizations have so often overlapped. Kaplan emphasized that fact by including special prayers in his prayer book that marked some of those special occasions on the American calendar for he firmly believed they were worthy of religious recognition.

But since religion was only part of our civilization, one could choose to worship in an Orthodox, Conservative or Reform synagogue – wherever one was most comfortable. It was not his intention to create a new movement although ultimately it came to that; only to provide an approach to Jewish life which allowed one to function within one's own movement and yet to be respectful of how others chose to identify. Kaplan, who was himself an observant Jew though for reasons far removed from Orthodox theology, made it possible for Reform Jews to become more observant for an entirely new set of reasons. We could affirm ritual to a greater or lesser extent not because we believed God commanded us as in Orthodoxy, or even just because we found it meaningful. Rather it was part of our civilization. It would it help to strengthen our Jewish ties to one another and to Jews around the world and would help to insure our survival as a people. The way we acted outwardly as Jews was after all not only significant in demonstrating who we were but also a way of giving expression to our values.

Kaplan's aim was to *reconstruct* Judaism as the Civilization of the Jewish People. In so far as he influenced me and many of my contemporaries who were in the process of becoming leaders in the Jewish world, his teaching was a great success. While the average Jew is probably not even familiar with Kaplan's name, and although we may not acknowledge it or realize it, we have in our way, as someone once observed, all become Reconstructionists. I am confident that later day historians will give appropriate credit to Mordecai Kaplan for his extraordinary contribution to the Jewish life of the twentieth century.

My four-and-a-half-years in Garden City were truly satisfying, both for Brenda and me and I believe for the congregation as well. While we were close to home and family and to many of the friends with whom we had grown up, we met wonderful people during those years, some still our friends years later. Brenda and I lived in an elegant house which the synagogue bought for us as a parsonage, only blocks from the temple. I used to walk to *shul* on Saturday mornings taking Evan with me as soon as he was old enough to sit through the service. What a wonderful experience that was. We always had a minyan on Saturday and on festival days even though attendance was better on Friday night. During the High Holidays we were packed.

It was during our days in Garden City that I built my first *sukkah* in the back yard of our house, evoking the warm memories which that holiday held for me. I banged my thumb as I hammered in the nails and held it up for display at services a day or two later as evidence of the *mitzvah* which I had so proudly performed. Less joyful was the special service we held to memorialize President Jack Kennedy. I was in the middle of writing my sermon for the evening on that Friday morning, baby sitting while Brenda went to the beauty parlor, which is still her Friday custom to this day. Needless to say, the subject of the sermon changed, but as with the death of FDR (when I was only twelve), I shall forever remember where I was and what I was doing when I first heard the tragic news which was to be a turning point in the history of this land.

There is one other memory I would share involving those halcyon days. It was in Garden City that I developed my real antipathy for Halloween. While Evan was still very young, we had dinner at 6 PM and he was asleep before or soon thereafter. Along would come the *Trick or Treaters* and not only disturb our meal but the ring of the doorbell would awaken him making it hard to get him back to sleep. So I wrote a letter to the local newspaper, *Newsday*, giving expression to my frustration and asking why it was that we were teaching our middle class children to beg given the sad reality that poverty was a scourge and begging a necessity for some in order to eat. I suggested that there were better values we could be teaching our children and also gave a sermon on the same subject on that Sabbath pointing out why I felt Halloween was not a very Jewish experience. In addition to the other reasons, did we not, after all, have our *Purim*?

Need I say the letters to the editor several days later were unkind at best? Downright nasty and bordering on being anti-Semitic would be more accurate. I was the Grinch who wanted to steal Halloween from their children. I haven't changed my views many years later although in the interest of full disclosure, I must admit that my own children made a big deal out of Halloween when their children were young. So much for parental influence! Or perhaps it was just their way of acknowledging the Kaplanian truth that we do indeed live in two civilizations.

There was an increase in membership during my tenure in Garden City. From the eighty or so families when I came, we became one hundred ten. Along with the Congregation, our family also grew. Jonathan Meir was born on January 10, 1966. His *Brit Milah* took place in the parsonage with many members present together with our parents who were by now also members of our congregation. By this time Evan was in Nursery School and somewhat unsure as to how to welcome his new brother. It was one of the rare times that he acted out in a way that was quite unlike him. Today, many years later, they are happily good friends though they live many miles apart.

THE JOURNEY TURNS SOUTH: A CONGREGATION CALLS

So now we had two sons and needed to think about our financial future. With all of the best intentions, and with all that was good about it, the Garden City Jewish Center was not going to be able to sustain us into future years. Fortuitously, my mentor Herbert Baumgard was again to play a significant role in my life. He had made the move to South Florida in 1956 as I entered my second year of seminary to become the director of the Southeast Region of the Union of American Hebrew Congregations from which position he oversaw all of the Reform congregations in the area as well as helping to birth new congregations. Thus, he was in a position to give me first hand information about Temple Sinai, a congregation he had helped found. It had just sold its building behind the North Miami Motor Pool to the Ivan Tors Movie Studio, released its second rabbi and was seeking a replacement. With money realized from the sale, it had purchased six tree-shaded acres with freely roaming peacocks along the Oleta River, at the northern end of Greynolds Park in a residential area called Sky Lake, part of a growing suburban area of Miami Dade County called North Miami Beach. Even as they embarked on a search for another rabbi and prepared for a new beginning, the congregation engaged an architect to draft plans for a sanctuary. My spiritual journey was again to take a new turn.

Rabbi Baumgard encouraged me to apply. It would be a good fit for me. The congregation had been classically Reform but apparently, some among its 150 families, including their president, were open to its becoming more traditional believing, correctly as it turned out, that this was to be the future direction of Reform Judaism. The growth potential was great and despite or perhaps because of the many challenges that newness offered, it would provide an opportunity for its next rabbi to truly leave his imprint. So, remembering also that the climate of Miami was not unlike that of the Philippines of which we had become quite fond, I submitted my name to the placement commission of the Central Conference of American Rabbis and awaited a response.

In August of 1966, on a Saturday morning while I was in synagogue, Sam Bloom, the chair of the pulpit committee called and invited us (the congregation wanted to meet Brenda as well) to come to Miami for an interview. Unlike the GCJC, Temple Sinai had a Sabbath morning service only when there was a Bar Mitzvah, so the expectation was that the rabbi would be at home which, of course, I wasn't, as Brenda explained to him much to his embarrassment. That remained a standing joke between Sam and me which neither of us ever forgot. Sam became a Saturday morning regular as soon as we initiated Sabbath morning worship and attended services and Torah study until he died at age 97.

I informed one of our GCJC board members of our plan, as required by our rabbinic Code of Ethics, asking him to please keep the matter confidential, requested both sets of grandparents to watch our children, and made arrangements to travel south with Brenda. We were met at the airport by members of the search committee, given a quick tour of Miami where the August sun was ablaze, and delivered to the old Balmoral Hotel on Collins Ave. in Bal Harbour where we settled into a lovely room.

Soon thereafter the whirlwind interview process began. We met with the search committee, with the board, with small groups of prominent members, and were wined and dined as well as interrogated. On Friday night, I conducted Sabbath Eve Services and on Saturday morning, one of the members drove us all the way south to Temple Beth Am in Kendall where Herbert Baumgard was the Rabbi (a position he held in addition to being Regional Director for the UAHC) so we could attend services and say hello. That Saturday night, we were introduced at a major social event celebrating the tenth anniversary of the congregation, which, by chance, had been planned for that very weekend. By the time we returned home we were quite exhausted. But not long thereafter, we received two phone calls which would change our lives. The first, after *Rosh Hashana*, informed us that the board had accepted the recommendation of the search committee and was calling a congregational meeting on the Sunday after *Yom Kippur* to ratify my selection as Rabbi of Temple Sinai. The second, after *Yom Kippur*, informed us that I had been selected almost unanimously, by the membership of the Temple to become its third rabbi and that everyone anxiously looked forward to our arrival.

The only issue that had raised some questions among the devotees of that classical Reform style with which the congregation had begun was the fact that I conducted services the weekend of my interview wearing a *yarmulke* and a *talit*. When asked about that by those who were accustomed to seeing their rabbis bareheaded, I explained that it was my understanding of Reform Judaism that such matters were left to personal choice; that to insist that one must pray bareheaded was as much of a form of orthodoxy as to insist that one pray with a covered head. It was my choice to pray in the traditional manner. But at the same time, I added, while I would be happy if others wished to follow my example, I would never insist that everyone follow suit for that would be a violation of the freedom of choice that was so much at the heart of the Reform movement.

Six families were not able to accept my explanation and resigned before I arrived, but the issue of my wearing a *kippah* and *talit* did not come up again even though as a compromise for those who had to get used to the new look, I wore a pulpit hat and robe during the first years because that looked like part of a uniform. I had no problem with that so long as I could cover my head. And I kept my word throughout the years never insisting that someone had to wear a *kippah* even though, as the years went on, more and more men opted to cover their heads during worship. That notwithstanding, the need to teach just what Reform Judaism was all about did occupy much time during the early years of my rabbinate in Temple Sinai as I will explain later.

When I made known my intention to leave the GCJC, most of our friends, while sad that we were leaving, understood. But among several of the leaders, there was anger. Even though there was nothing in writing, and although I had given the necessary four months notice as required by the Rabbinic Placement Commission which supported and in fact encouraged my decision, they felt I had gone back on my word which was that I would stay at least for another year. They were, of course, not entirely wrong. In their eyes, I was not only violating a contract but jilting them, as if for different lover, an emotion not uncommon when a rabbi leaves one congregation for another, the more so when it is in mid-year. But I truly believed, as I said in my farewell sermon, that I was more needed by the people in North Miami Beach than I was in Garden City; that I had done the best I could over four and a half years but that it was necessary for my family and me to move on to a new challenge.

Moreover, my call to Temple Sinai was contingent on my arrival there as soon as possible. Its members were not even happy about having to wait until February, the agreed upon date of my arrival, for they were without leadership and stability. I wish that those who accused me of betrayal might have better understood that this was a special opportunity for me which might not arise again for several years if ever and that sometimes, one needed to make choices that were not all black or white. The result, sadly, was that there was never a proper saying goodbye, no celebratory farewell party to mark our parting; only two final Sabbath Services prior to our leaving on a snowy Saturday night, Feb. 11, 1967.

Happily, the anger softened over the years and even turned to pride when it became evident what I was accomplishing in North Miami Beach. There were frequent visits by members of the GCJC to Temple Sinai when they visited South Florida or when they moved here. And on those occasions when we would return to our former congregation while visiting New York, we were always warmly welcomed. Time and reflection have a way of healing old wounds.

In truth, those four-and- a-half-years were very special. Exciting as the prospect of moving was, I did not leave without a feeling of sadness. This, after all, had been my first full time congregation: where I had begun to put into practice what my teachers had taught me at HUC-JIR and where I could begin to actualize a philosophy of Jewish life– to write my spiritual plan book, if you will. It was also where the four of us– Brenda, Evan, Jonathan and I-- celebrated the cycle of the Jewish year, where we sat around the Sabbath table each Friday night and where I first began to pronounce the priestly blessing upon my sons as is customary for Jewish parents to do; where we dressed in costume for *Purim* and built our first *Sukkah*. I was almost tearful when I realized that February 3rd would be our last regular Shabbat dinner in Garden City. The movers were to come the following week and then, after one more Shabbat marked by a farewell sermon on Friday night and one more Bat Mitzvah on Feb. 11th, we would be would be gone. Four and a half years would become a memory.

Once the movers came, we moved in with Brenda's parents for our final days in New York. We timed our move so that the Moving Van would meet us when we arrived in Miami and determined that we would leave New York as the Sabbath ended allowing the rhythm of Jewish life to mirror what was going on in our lives: beginning our journey even as the old week ended and a new week began; marking the end of an important period in our development while looking ahead to a new challenge. In the presence of both sets of parents and not without a few tears, we recited *Havdallah*, the prayer of separation between the Sabbath and the weekdays very aware that this was also a separation of a more permanent kind. We said our goodbyes and packed ourselves, our two children and our dachshund Akiba, whom we had brought from the Philippines, into our Pontiac Trans Am convertible, and embarked on the journey to our new land of promise. The three stars which marked the start of a new week were not visible for the snow was falling lightly as we drove off into the darkness of the night. But before us we knew there would be warmth and the brightness of the sun.

TEMPLE SINAI:
THE EARLY DAYS

T he welcome we received on the following Sabbath Eve was generous and enthusiastic. One hundred and fifty people of all ages squeezed into a small auditorium in back of the Washington Federal Bank, off a busy North Miami Beach street. Services were held there while the architectural firm of Russell-Melton Associates began to envision what a sanctuary might look like on the recently- acquired grounds of the former Greynold's Stable along the banks of the Oleta River, site of the new synagogue. The Auditorium was of course completely inadequate but it was to serve us for Sabbath and Holiday worship except for the High Holidays when we rented the North Miami Beach Civic Auditorium. It was not until two years later, in the Spring of 1969, that we were to march in procession through the streets of North Miami Beach to our almost completed new building, singing, while carrying two Torah scrolls in our arms, so that we could celebrate *Shavuot* in our new sanctuary.

I set forth my spiritual agenda that night and as I look back on my years at Temple Sinai, I am amazed at how unwavering I was in its pursuit. I also understand now what my teacher Dr. Henry Slonimsky meant when he once told us in class that a rabbi preaches only one sermon during his lifetime, with weekly variations on a theme. He was right.

During the early years of my rabbinate, I had begun to be drawn to the writings of the so called "covenant theologians" within the Reform movement: among others, men like Eugene Borowitz and Arnold Jacob Wolf. I had met Gene Borowitz at the first NFTY Kallah (like a conclave except that the emphasis was more on serious study than on socialization) while he was still a pulpit rabbi before he became a Professor at HUC-JIR. He introduced the twenty or so of us who attended to the teaching of Martin Buber, who taught that the ideal human relationship was one in which human beings treated each other as subjects rather than objects- as an *I to a Thou*, rather than an *I to It*. For Buber, God was the *Eternal Thou* whom we could discover as we related to a human thou.

Arnold Wolf, a very creative and controversial rabbi from Chicago spoke of the need to be radical and traditional at the same time -- radical in pursuit of a social justice agenda and traditional in religious practice. Both Wolf and Borowitz, and those who were of like-mind sought to make the idea of *mitzvah,* a term ignored by the classical Reform thinkers, fashionable again. They spoke of being open to hearing God's call to us, even as they affirmed the autonomy of the individual to make Jewish choices, albeit within bounds of the tradition. Most of all, they taught the necessity of taking the tradition seriously, a message that had taken hold in my mind and was to accompany me throughout my years as a rabbi.

Thus, it was against that background that I chose to speak of three *mitzvot* or imperatives that I deemed essential if we were to succeed as a congregation: making worship come alive so that it would become more than words on the pages of a prayer book; engagement with the world and the pursuit of righteous acts through what, in the Reform movement, was then known as Social Action, now referred to as *Tikun Olam* (repairing our world); and engaging in Jewish study on all levels in a serious way.

Among my first achievements was the introduction of a regular Sabbath morning service. Sad to say, many Reform congregations, Temple Sinai then among them, had a Sabbath morning service only in the event of a *Bar* or *Bat Mitzvah*. (The latter, incidentally, was still rare in those days since girls were not required or expected to learn Hebrew). But, I argued, would the congregation be happy if I, whose custom it was to go to synagogue on Saturday morning, would be forced to go to a Conservative Temple in the neighborhood? The point having been made, we started having Sabbath services during my second week in North Miami Beach and have never missed a *minyan* (the quorum of ten Jews required for communal prayer) since.

Of course, there were those for whom my innovations were sure signs of the congregation's turn to Conservative Judaism if not to Orthodoxy. The fact that I wore *yarmulke* and *tallit* and encouraged *Bnai Mitzvah* to follow suit, introduced more Hebrew into the service even asking those gathered to stand for the *Ameedah* (it was after all the *Standing Prayer*), and encouraged the chanting of Torah and *Haftarah*, were all seen as sure signs of the abandonment of Reform. In addition, after a year or so I took off my robe for to me it meant being separated from the people rather than being just another Jew at prayer who happened simply to be better educated Jewishly than most others. I also stopped raising my hands when I offered the closing benediction for while I had grown up with that custom, I laid claim to no priestly powers.

Happily, most were pleased by what was happening which, as it turns out, was exactly the direction The Reform movement was to follow. In fact, I am proud to say we were and continued to be several steps ahead of the curve as Reform Judaism engaged in its own journey back towards tradition. And while much of my energy during those early years was spent educating the congregation in what I believed Reform was all about, and while we lost a few die hard old line Reformers, we began to attract new members who liked the direction the congregation had begun to take. As a result, the congregation grew and the need for a permanent home became more urgent.

Now that I was on the scene, I could offer my vision of what a sanctuary should be like at firsthand rather than from afar. In keeping with my view of worship, it was important to me that the sanctuary not be proscenium style like a theater with the rabbi appearing like an actor on a stage in front of an audience. Rather there needed to be an intimate feel with everyone experiencing a feeling of closeness. It was to be more like theater in the round except that prayer was to be experienced by a community that shared a common bond, all of whom were in search of a spiritual experience; not by a group of strangers gathered to be entertained. Our architects, Russell–Melton Associates were wonderful to work with. They did their homework and crafted a beautiful plan; a sanctuary whose seats wrapped around the *Bema* and whose ceiling soared upward into the heavens. The front focus was a sixty foot tower which was to hold the Holy Ark and light was to come in from the outside through clear glass panels so that we could see our beautiful surroundings, especially the trees.

When the sanctuary was being positioned on our property during the early design stage, the architects informed us that following the tradition that prayers should be directed to the East (towards Jerusalem) would mean having to uproot and destroy some stately old trees, while turning the building slightly northward would mean saving those trees. What might we want them to do? Unanimously we agreed that God would happily forego our following the custom of facing toward Jerusalem if it meant saving God's creation.

We had also agreed that, contrary to more common custom, we would build our sanctuary before we built a school building, important as education was in Jewish life. Our thought was that we needed a place to pray not only to fill the needs of our members for whom worship was important but also to attract new members. Classrooms were available to us in a local junior high school (JFK) and would tide us over till we could afford a school. On the other hand, if we built the school first, we might have less incentive to build a sanctuary. It turns out that we made the absolutely correct decision. In point of fact, we only had to wait four years after the completion of the sanctuary before we had our school building, the first of many building projects which were to occupy us in the years to come.

As we went about approving plans for the sanctuary, we also undertook the task of raising the necessary funds to pay for it, the first of many fund drives with which I was to be involved. We had no major contributors so we borrowed the money by selling first mortgage bonds which paid a return of 6.5%. Our hope was that when the bonds matured, people might contribute them instead of reclaiming their principle. In any case, they came due in staggered periods so we had some time to worry about how they would be repaid. As it happened, our largest bondholder, Henry Perlman, died of old age not long after he had purchased $86,000 and willed his bonds to Temple Sinai. You can imagine that his death evoked a certain amount of mixed emotions. We were naturally saddened by his passing but our building was to cost us $360,000 so his bequest represented almost one fourth. Money was always a problem, as it is for most religious institutions, yet somehow, we always managed to pay our bills.

It was exciting to watch the building rise up on our beautiful property aside the Oleta River. First the concrete foundation was poured. Then we waited somewhat impatiently for the wood which had to be transported all the way from Alabama. We cheered when the trucks finally arrived and watched in awe as the majestic beams were placed so that they soared heavenward, each fitting into the other as if by some divine plan. The coral rock which constituted the walls came from closer to home in Florida. The excitement built as each day brought us closer to the time we would actually be able to move in. It might have been sooner but, following the model of the building of the portable Temple in the wilderness in the time of Moses and in conformity with Jewish law, we instructed the workmen that they were not to work on the Sabbath.

At last that day came when we could bring our two Torah scrolls into the newly completed sanctuary. On a somewhat overcast afternoon in the spring of 1969, after Sunday School, children and adults of all ages, gathered in front of the Washington Federal Bank auditorium where we had been holding Sabbath Services for the last two years and marched the mile and a half or two to the new Temple, holding the scrolls and flags left over from *Simchat Torah*, and singing Hebrew songs. It was a powerful and memorable moment for all who participated. The floor was still unfinished and the pews were not yet installed, but we wanted to accommodate one of our founding families whose son was to become *Bar Mitzvah* the following weekend. And so a new era for Temple Sinai began. I was to preside at services in a beautiful sanctuary that, in my view, still has no equal. It came as no surprise some months later that its design had gained national recognition and that the architects were given an award.

In my Rosh Hashana sermon that year titled *Sermons in Stones: the Meaning of a Building*, I tried to show how the architecture of our new building was a reflection of the values which we held dear. The use of stone and wood, materials of the earth, reflected the fact that we Jews are an earthbound people who care deeply about what happens in and to our world and to its inhabitants. At the same time, the soaring roof reminded us to reach towards that which is above and beyond our grasp, to that *Power not ourselves* we call God. And all the time, even as we experience the tension between heaven and earth, between that which is and that which might be, the eyes of the worshipper are drawn towards the Ark in which is kept the very source of our values, our sacred Torah scroll. Even those who were not accustomed to praying with any regularity could not help but be moved by the beauty and the power of our sanctuary.

We waited until the following fall to officially dedicate our new building, by which time its interior was more complete. It happened that the Union of American Hebrew Congregations Biennial Convention was held on Miami Beach that year so I was able to prevail on another of my rabbinic heroes, to act as the dedication speaker- one of the great preachers and rabbinic exemplars of the Reform movement, Rabbi Jacob Phillip Rudin. He was going to attend the Biennial and thus be close by saving us both the expense of housing and transportation. In addition to having been from the neighboring community of Great Neck when I was in Garden City, his wife was also distantly related to my wife Brenda which made his presence even more special. We didn't know it then, but he also had a home in the Berkshires which was to serve as an inspiration to Brenda and me in later years when we began to think about buying a second home and spending our summers there. Alas, there are not many men of like stature who still walk in our midst today. He had a way with words which few could match and a true *Yiddishe Neshuma*, a deeply feeling Jewish soul.

It was at that same time that we also began to search for an Ark which would do justice to our otherwise magnificent sanctuary. We had run out of money and had made use of the same portable Ark that had served the congregation during its recent years of wandering. But now the time had come to fill the *Bema* tower with something more in keeping with its majesty. After all, the reading and study of Torah was for me the most central part of Sabbath morning worship. In addition to chanting the Torah, to which the congregation had not been accustomed, and engaging in Torah study before the reading, I had also re-introduced the custom of a Torah procession know as a *HaKafah* on Saturday morning, when the Torah was removed from the Ark. It had long been forsworn in Reform congregations except for *Simhat Torah*. But the Torah, after all, belonged to the people and was not the sole possession of the rabbi. Hence it needed to be brought down from the *Bema* into the congregation.

Since the UAHC Biennial encouraged Jewish artisans to set up booths both for self-promotion and to sell their wares to the several thousand delegates attending from all around the country, Brenda and I walked through the display galleries at the convention hotel in search. I knew that Solomon's Temple was made of wood and stone and metal. Our new building had wood and stone but the metal was missing so we looked for someone who might be able to fill that void; someone who could create an Ark for us that would be worthy of the space allocated for it by the architect.

Amazingly, as if by divine direction, we came upon an impish little man with a bright red beard who was from Hollywood, California. His name was Yosef Pelzig and he worked in metal. It was love at first sight! We quickly invited him to come with us to the Temple so that we could show him our sanctuary and specifically the *Bema* tower which was to house the *Aron Kodesh*. So began the process which resulted in an Ark that is as unique as it is beautiful.

In the old *Union Prayer Book*, (official prayer book of the Reform movement until it was succeeded by *The Gates of Prayer* in 1975) the words of Psalm 24, *S'u Sh'arim Rosheichem...Lift up your heads O ye gates...* introduced the Torah service, and was sung when the Torah was taken from the Ark and brought into the congregation where it was to be read. It was those words which kept floating around in my head. Couldn't we somehow create gates which would rise up as we prepared to remove the Torah from the Ark, reflecting the words of the Psalm which in turn must have been a reflection of Temple days in Jerusalem? My idea was not very practical, but Pelzig did come up with the concept of metal gates which were to be attached to the frame of the *Bema* tower and would swing open and shut. Brilliant and very doable!

Pelzig sent us a design after he returned to California. The gates, one for each side, would be about ten feet tall and each would be in the design of a seven branched *menorah* enhanced by other seasonal symbols such as a decanter of wine (*Shabbat*), clusters of grapes (*Sukkot*) and sheaves of wheat (*Shavuot*). He also designed an Eternal Light which would hang above the doors, thus transforming the entire *Bema* tower into a walk-in Ark. The Torah scrolls would be set on shelves attached to the coral rock walls and would be screened by see through linen on the back of the doors. Natural light would continue to flow in through the clear glass windows at the top of the *Bema* tower enhanced by interior flood lights which would highlight the scrolls and also provide lighting at night. I submitted the design to the board which enthusiastically approved the idea. It remained only for me to find a way to pay for it. Six families responded to my appeal and became the *Bnai Aron Kodesh (Children of the Holy Ark)*, each with a pledge of $5000.

The new Ark which continues to be the envy of all who see it was in place by the following *Rosh Hashana*. Yosef Pelzig himself accompanied the shipment from California and installed it. With very little help, standing on a small ladder and working like the consummate artisan that he was, he made sure that every bolt was in its place and that the doors swung easily and closed in a proper manner. As I recall those several days during which he stayed in a small dinky motel a mile or so from Temple Sinai, and worked into the night to make sure he would finish on time, I am amazed at how smoothly the work progressed and how extraordinary were the gifts of this little man who was, in my eyes, a modern day Bezalel. Like the name of his biblical ancestor who designed and built the portable Temple which accompanied the Israelites through the wilderness, he too stood as if in the *shadow of the Divine*.

THE SEARCH FOR A CANTOR AND MORE CHANGE

B ut important as was the Ark in creating a spiritual environment, it was clear that more was required. The musical portions of our worship were lagging. When I first arrived we had a lay cantor-- a member of the congregation who had a beautiful voice but who, in addition to being nearly blind, was unable to read Hebrew and had very little knowledge of classical Jewish music beyond the very limited prayer book responses which he had memorized. He was followed by a cantor who was schooled in the Conservative musical tradition, with little feeling for what was expected of a cantor in a more liberal setting. Nor did he have a particularly engaging voice. The time had clearly come for us to embark on a search for a cantor, one who not only had an outstanding voice but who was trained in the traditions of the Reform synagogue. He would need to have collateral skills as a Jewish educator as well since we were not able, at that time, to afford someone who would only sing on the Sabbath and on holidays.

So it is that after an intensive search we engaged Cantor Irving Shulkes, who was to remain my colleague until the day we both retired, twenty eight years later. Together we created a musical environment at Temple Sinai that became the envy of all who worshipped with us. We were able to transform the somewhat formal and hymn-like music of the early Reform movement into a joyful expression of song and prayer directed to the Holy One of Blessing, in keeping with the vision of music during worship which I had begun to develop. Although our musical tastes did not always coincide, especially in the later years when Jewish modes of worship and musical styles began to change, our sanctuary never lacked for *the sound of music.*

One of my greatest joys was in officiating at Irving's wedding to Joanne Serisky, a single mother whom he met when she volunteered for his choir. Needless to say, the *Bema* was filled with music on that *Erev Hanukah* in 1977 when what seemed like an army of cantors stood beneath the *Chupah* with the bride and groom and me to chant the *Shevah Brachot*- the seven marriage blessings. None who were present then will ever forget the experience. In keeping with the *Hanukah* theme, since some believed that Irving would never marry, I quipped: *A great miracle happened here* during my wedding talk. In time, Joanne would give birth to Heather, who is today herself a mother, having also been married on the same *Bema*, beneath the same *Chupah* as her parents.

As we attracted more people who wanted to become part of Temple Sinai, many of whom had come from more traditional congregations but were very comfortable with our style of Judaism, there also came questions about our practices. Why, for example, did we only observe one day of *Rosh Hashanah* when most Jews, except for those in Reform congregations, observed two?

There was of course a historical reason. The Jews of the ancient Diaspora (Babylonia) were uncertain as to the exact time a festival began because they depended on the word coming from Jerusalem after the Sanhedrin declared the festival to have begun. They therefore added an extra day at the beginning and at the end of certain festival days in order to make sure they observed each holiday at the right time and for the correct number of days. Thus *Rosh Hashanah* became a two day holiday even though the Torah allows for only one day. By the time of *Yom Kippur*, the last of the *Ten Days of Awe*, the exact time was known and there was no need to observe it for two days; nor would a two-day fast have been acceptable. But, with the passing of the years and the beginning of Reform Judaism in the nineteenth century, the calendar had been set scientifically and no longer depended on the sighting of the moon in Jerusalem. Why keep a second day, therefore, the Reformers argued, quite cogently, and removed it from their practice.

Ralph and Brenda at their engagement and 50 years later.

Top: *A two year old "Rolf Peter Kissinger" with his parents Albert and Erna.*

Bottom: *Ralph Peter Kingsley and his parents on summer vacation in the Catskills six years later.*

The aspiring young actor in rehearsal, playing Demetrius in the Queens College production of MIDSUMMER NIGHT'S DREAM in 1951.

With classmates on the eve of ordination from HUC-JIR in 1960. Soon to be Rabbi Ralph is on the far right.

As a student Rabbi in Lindenhurst, LI conducting a Sabbath Eve Service.

With the insignia of the USAF Jewish Chaplain (10 Commandments) on his summer uniform-ready to serve in the Philippines.

The serious expression of a young rabbi in his pulpit hat and the smile of a retiree today.

With Torah in one hand and seven year old son Evan Moshe in the other, the rabbi of Temple Sinai leads a Torah Procession through the streets of North Miami Beach on the way to the new sanctuary in 1969.

Thanking President Carter at a White House Reception for P.M. and Mrs. Menachem Begin, 1978.

With his favorite congressman, William Lehman Sr. in 1983.

At the end of a different "journey," the third of five marathons.

At the grave of grandfather Isidor who died in Nuremberg. The stone also memorializes grandmother Else, a victim of the Holocaust whose grave is unknown and an aunt and uncle who were cremated.

At the Kissinger Reunion in Israel, 2008, Ralph and Brenda are in the third row up, to the right of center.

The Kingsley family with pet K'tonton in 1978. And significantly expanded at the Bar Mitzvah of grandson Max, in front of the Ark at Temple Sinai, in 2012.

But by 1971, times had changed. Not only was there an increased longing for a return to some of the practices that the Reformers had discarded, but a new State of Israel had come into being. While modern Israelis, Orthodox as well as Liberal, followed the biblical calendar (no additional days of *Yom Tov* as in the Diaspora) they did make one exception. That was *Rosh Hashanah* about which the ancient rabbis had decreed that it was to be observed for two days, even in Israel. With this in mind, a number of Reform synagogues, wanting to be in sync with what was happening in Israel, among other reasons, added a second day as well.

While I had grown up in the classical Reform tradition, my experiences both as a chaplain where I ministered to Jews from all steams of Judaism and as rabbi of the GCJC where two days was the custom, led me, in my personal practice, to adopt a second day. During my first several years in North Miami Beach, I continued that practice on the second day of *Rosh Hashanah* by going to a nearby Conservative temple where I was made to feel very welcome. Knowing what I knew and feeling what I felt, it was perfectly natural therefore that I should be receptive to the request that Temple Sinai make such observance part of its practice. Moreover, if ten Jews wanted to pray, were not we as a congregation and I as a rabbi, obliged to meet their needs?

So it was that we polled the membership and found that a significant enough number said they would come to make holding services on the second day of the Jewish New Year feasible. We therefore announced that there would be a service on that day, albeit only for *those who wished* so that it would not appear to be coercive or be guilt-inducing for those who felt that one day was sufficient. For me it was a *slam dunk* as they say. After all, offering a second day was totally in keeping with my philosophy of Reform Judaism which allowed for choice not only in what one could discard but in what one could add back. What I didn't know was that this was to become a flash point issue for some of the old school Reformers who were afraid that I was making the congregation Conservative and that they would be driven away. Of course there was no such intention but as *Rosh Hashanah* approached, I began to receive threatening calls warning of mass resignations, the withholding of funds and possibly the loss of my job.

Four years after coming to Temple Sinai, I was faced with a real crisis of conscience. Should I take the safe path by letting the voices of the nay-sayers prevail? Or should I risk my job by doing that which may not have been most prudent but was what I believed to be right? The Friday before the Monday of *Rosh Hashanah*, I worked on my sermon which dealt with the changing nature of Reform Judaism and how the Reform of 1971, after the Holocaust and after the rebirth of Israel was different from that of the early founders who were busy rejecting what they thought was preventing them from entering into the modern world. As times and needs had drastically changed over the years, so too must we, I would argue. But I still had not made up my mind how I would end it: With a capitulation and *we will get there but more slowly than I had wished* or, *therefore we will come together again on Tuesday?*

It was on that Friday night that I made my decision during a moment when the words of the prayer book truly spoke to me just as they were meant to. During the moment of silent prayer at the conclusion of the *Amidah,* I read *And when in Thy wisdom Thou sendest trials and sorrows, grant me strength to bear them patiently and courage to trust in Thy help.* When I looked up and out at the congregation, I realized that those who had called wanting me to keep Jews from praying on the second day of the holiday were not among those who came with any regularity to celebrate *Shabbat* while those for whom a second day would add to their religious experience filled the pews that night as they usually did every Sabbath eve. It was at that moment I made my decision. We would convene on the second day, regardless of the consequences. I announced it that night and again on the first day at the end of my sermon which I concluded by saying: *therefore we will have services tomorrow morning.* Much to my great delight, 400 people showed up on the second day, many of them for the first and only time in their lives. But they wanted to support me and so they were there. We have had a second day ever since, always with a respectable size congregation. The then president of the congregation, incidentally, made a point of publically announcing that he would <u>not</u>

be there, adding a bit more drama to the occasion. But unbeknownst to me at the time, he was going through some personal turmoil in his life so I forgave him although our relationship would never be the same. That was one of the turning points of my tenure at Temple Sinai. Another was to come in 1973 when Israel was attacked on *Yom Kippur*.

THE IMPACT OF ISRAEL

Israel the nation had not played much of a role during the formative years of my spiritual journey. It was seldom, if ever, a topic of discussion in my home. I was singularly unaware of that extraordinary moment on Nov. 29, 1947 when the UN General Assembly voted 33-13 in favor of a Partition Plan which was to lead to the establishment of an Arab and a Jewish state in what was then known as Palestine. The even more spectacular events of May 14 (the 5th of Iyar) 1948 also left no lasting impression. That was when, upon the final departure of British occupying soldiers, the man who was to be the first Prime Minister of Israel, David Ben Gurion, read a masterful Declaration of Independence thus giving birth to the new State of Israel. I have vague earlier recollections of having brought home a JNF (Jewish National Fund) can to collect pennies for the purpose of planting trees in Palestine as all Sunday School children were expected to do during those days, but I was, after all, not even thirteen years old so what did it mean to me given the fact of my very minimal Jewish upbringing?

We sang Zionist songs about the pioneering spirit in Israel during my NFTY (The National Federation of Temple Youth) days but we were much more engaged with the cause of civil rights than with the trials and tribulations of that new born land. The Classical Reform Judaism of my youth was much more interested in the social justice message of the Hebrew prophets than in the struggle to create a Jewish homeland. Even the fact that Rabbi Stephen S. Wise, one of the great Zionists of the twentieth century (some argue the greatest), had founded my seminary, the Jewish Institute of Religion, in 1922 because the Liberal Hebrew Union College in Cincinnati was at the very least non- Zionist if not Anti- Zionist, did not result in a great emphasis on Zionist ideology; or the importance of Israel to the future of Judaism and the Jewish People, for that matter. If it did, it passed me by.

It was only in June 1967, soon after I had assumed the pulpit of Temple Sinai that I began to understand how critical Israel was to Jewish survival. While at HUC-JIR, I had studied the writings of Achad HaAm and his cultural Zionism (as opposed to political Zionism) which saw Israel as being the place in which authentic Jewish life and creativity would spring forth from a population that was largely Jewish. I had also come to understand how important Israel was in the teachings of Mordecai Kaplan, who relied heavily on Achad HaAm for the development of his Reconstructionist philosophy and for whom Israel was a central focus of the Jewish civilization. During my days in Garden City, I had made my first modest gift to the United Jewish Appeal in support of Israel at the annual congregational breakfast. But it was not until Israel came under attack during the Six Days War that I recognized, as did so many in the Jewish world, that not much more than twenty years after the slaughter of six million Jews, there was, yet again, an existential attack against not only the newly developing Jewish State but against the Jewish people as well. If Israel did not prevail, we might well all face another Holocaust; there might no longer be a Jewish people.

Prevail of course we did. We had learned our lesson after having stood silently by along with the rest of the world while six million Jews were murdered during World War ll. Guided by now well organized professionals in the Jewish Federation and led by rabbis and devoted Jewish laypeople, our Jewish community (and communities throughout the land), quickly mobilized, raising significant sums of money, even from Jews who had been very peripheral in their involvement, and enlisting the aid and support of as many influential people as possible in the media, in Washington and in the non-Jewish world.

Despite our efforts over the post war years to engage in inter-faith dialogue, however, Christian churches and their ministers, disappointed us. They simply could not or would not understand what we were going through. As a result, we learned that the only people we could safely rely on to help us in times of crisis was ourselves, which led to a reenergized American Jewish community. It created a new mantra that would remain with us for many years: *Never again. Never again* would Jews remain silent in the face of adversity. *Never again* would we allow ourselves to be victimized without fighting back. *Never again* would we allow an attack against our people anywhere in the world but especially in Israel to go unanswered. *Never again* would we expect others to do battle for us. It wasn't going to happen.

That reenergized community changed its priorities placing Israel at the top of the list of its concerns even as we came to a deeper understanding of the famous teaching of the ancient sage Hillel: *If I am not for myself, who will be for me?* As a result of the miraculous victory which took place during those six short days, there was a renewed interest in Israel which resulted in a deepening of Jewish consciousness, a greater interest in Hebrew, no longer an archaic tongue but a living language, and a desire for more Jewish learning. After all, if Israel was to become a laboratory for Jewish culture where a Jew could live a fully Jewish life, where the cycle of the Jewish year did not depend on the work habits of the non Jewish population, where the day of rest was Saturday not Sunday, shouldn't we take greater advantage of what was happening there? And that did not even take into account the deeper understanding of Israel as a place for the ingathering of exiles where every Jew could find a home and lay claim to a place of his or her own.

Indeed, the historic anti-Zionist position of the Reform movement prior to WW2 which had given way at first to a non-Zionist position (i.e. no longer anti) in the 1940s and had changed to a modestly pro-Zionist stance after 1948, now became fervently pro Israel. We sent our children to study programs in Israel, began to sponsor congregational trips to the *land of our forebears* and brought young emissaries (*shlichim*) from there to visit our Jewish camps and our schools. The entire mood and tone had begun to change. For the first time in 1970, the Reform rabbinic body, The Central Conference of American Rabbis, held its annual convention in Jerusalem and voted to do so every seventh year thereafter. It would be a major turning point, a change in the life of the

Reform movement and in my spiritual life as a Jew as well. For no Jew, once having set foot in Israel, ever emerges quite the same as he or she had been before. More about this later.

By 1973 our commitment to Israel had become normative and I had decided, as a personal decision, to devote at least one sermon to Israel each year during the High Holidays, usually on *Yom Kippur* morning. That year, as I was preparing to begin the *Yom Kippur* morning service (I had just concluded leading the children's service and was catching my breath) one of our congregants came in to the robing area behind the *Bemah* and informed me that Israel had been attacked from several sides by Arab armies. This time, unlike 1967, the initiative came from the other side and Israel, having been caught by surprise, was sustaining heavy losses. Again, her very life and that of its inhabitants was imperiled.

Services continued throughout the day but transistor radios (before the days of i-Phones) in the hands of congregants kept us informed of what was going on. Needless to say it was an extra emotional time for us all. The prayers spoke to us in a very special way, especially when we sang *B'Rosh Hashanah Y'kateivu U'V'Yom Tzom Kippur Y'chateimu, Mi Yamut U'mi Y'ch'yeh...On Rosh Hashanah it is written and on Yom Kippur it is sealed, who shall live and who shall die...* It was truly such a life and death moment not only for the State of Israel but for the Jewish People.

By the time three stars appeared in the sky to mark the end of the day, the Jewish community, in crisis mode, had begun to mobilize. We, at Temple Sinai, made plans to hold a major fund raising event on behalf of Israel during the following week but we did not wait for that event to take place. Even before that event, Kenny Schwartz, then synagogue President and subsequently my life-long friend, his wife Maxine who learned her first aleph bet from me around that time and later became an outstanding Hebraist and Jewish leader, and I, took our act on the road. We went to the condominiums in which many of our members resided and held fund raising meetings. Money was needed to support Israel's economy which had ground to a halt while her citizen army was once again engaged, in fighting the surrounding Arab nations which had launched so scurrilous an attack on an unsuspecting nation during its most sacred day of the year. All of our efforts were coordinated by The Greater Miami Jewish Federation which had become even better organized since the time of the Six Days War. It had become a major force, alongside the synagogues, in providing leadership for the Jewish community, especially in time of crisis. We, too, though a relatively young congregation, were proudly to come of age during those days and took our place among the more established congregations of Greater Miami.

YEARS OF GROWTH

By now, four years after we had moved into our new sanctuary and two years after the trauma of adding a second day of *Rosh Hashanah* had faded into the background, the congregation was growing in numbers and in financial strength. Young families were not only adding to our membership but were assuming leadership roles in the congregation as well. A new building providing much-needed space to accommodate our expanding Sunday school and mid-week Hebrew programs as well as housing the newly created Nursery school was nearing completion. And it would not come a moment too soon. In far from optimal circumstances, Hebrew classes were being held in classrooms provided by our neighbor, St. Lawrence Church, and the Nursery school had been temporarily meeting in the Social Hall where classes were separated by moveable partitions and teachers wrote on portable blackboards. While we appreciated the graciousness of our Catholic neighbor and have had a wonderful relationship with them over the years (its pastor and I preached from each other's pulpit on a number of occasions and we use their parking lot on the High Holidays and they ours on Easter and Christmas) we were less than comfortable with crosses on the classroom walls and were ready and anxious for a place of our own.

Plans were to dedicate the new building during *Hanukah* of that year, 1973. What more appropriate time could there be than the Festival of Dedication? It had been made possible by a $100,000 loan from an elderly couple without children, Irvin and Fanny Rosenblum. We were to pay them interest but the loan was to become a gift upon their death. Still, with all of the good things that were happening, there was not yet a real sense of cohesiveness within the congregation, a feeling of being united as a community.

In a strange way, the *Yom Kippur* War was to change that. When we gathered at night several days after the Day of Atonement, it was as with a singleness of purpose and a true sense of partnership for we were responding to an attack on our very existence. A congregation of disparate individuals who had joined, some because they believed in sustaining Jewish life, some because they needed to enroll their children in a Jewish school in preparation for *Bar* or *Bat Mitzvah*, some for purely social reasons, suddenly found themselves united by a deeper purpose. They had come to understand that the very future of Jewish life was threatened and that, therefore, what they did in response mattered. They opened their hearts to the challenge and their pocketbooks as well. And while I no longer recall the numbers, I know that during that evening we raised significant sums both for the Israel Emergency Fund and for the Israel Bond Organization. We discovered that the members of Temple Sinai were far more affluent as a group then we had known. Earlier attempts to encourage giving beyond minimum dues on a voluntary basis had not been very successful. But Israel at war had struck a chord and the money poured forth. It was an important moment in the development of the congregation and helped me to better understand the dynamics of Jewish life. The fact is that Jews respond best in time of crisis.

It should perhaps be noted here that it was during that time that I began to understand, as well, the importance of the Federation movement as an important piece in the fabric of Jewish life. There had been a time, certainly during my growing up years, that rabbis were called upon when it came time to provide leadership in the Jewish community. Wealthy Jews of the American Jewish Committee variety made their presence known in exerting influence behind the scenes as the self-appointed representatives of the Jewish populace in meeting with high government officials. But it was the rabbis, leaders of their synagogues, who helped mobilize the mass of Jews in times of crisis, and the rabbis who were quoted in the press on matters of Jewish concern; who gave expression to the voice of the greater Jewish community. Indeed, one might say, without fear of contradiction, that the rabbis exerted power by virtue of what they represented even more than by virtue of who they were.

Not surprisingly therefore, it was we rabbis who were asked, literally, to *hit the road* to raise funds on behalf of our beloved Israel whose very life hung in the balance. So desperate was the situation that two traditional colleagues from neighboring congregations, Rabbis Max Lipschitz and Milton Schlinsky, both of blessed memory, who normally would never have driven on *Yom Tov*, got in the car with me (I was the *Shabbos goy*) on *Sukkot* afternoon. We three drove to one of the local hospitals to raise money from our Jewish doctors believing we needed to meet them where they were. This was clearly for the sake of saving lives for which one may violate the holiest commandment. It was a bittersweet moment that I recall with great fondness for them both.

But, more generally, the balance of power had begun to slowly shift during the years following World War II and by the time of the Six Days War, it was clear that a new leadership paradigm was beginning to emerge. It was newly energized Jewish laymen who were making decisions as leaders of the United Jewish Appeal and Jewish Federations. To be sure, it was their giving ability that helped place these laymen in positions of influence, but clearly, incidents such as that described above notwithstanding, the power of the rabbis in the overall scheme of things had begun to diminish.

I mention that not by way of criticism but as reflective of a new emerging reality and because it led to another consequence: a certain competition between the synagogue, on the one hand, and the Jewish Federation on the other. Which one was the true representative of the Jewish community, not only when it came to giving voice to Jewish needs and concerns but also when it came to a competition for Jewish dollars? As Federations grew in the scope of their activities and in their influence, there was a fear in the minds of some rabbis that support of Federation would siphon away dollars and thus have a negative impact on the health of their synagogue. There were times when I myself harbored such fears. But in point of fact, the exact opposite was true, and the heroic events of 1967 and even more those of 1973 taught me that lesson. Far from being adversaries during those trauma filled days, there arose a new symbiosis between the two institutions with each one understanding its reliance on the other as they worked together for the survival of the Jewish people. Not only that, but I was to realize that once a person learns to give, his or her synagogue will be as much the beneficiary as will the Federation.

That was exactly our experience in 1973 when we came to Israel's aid. As a result of our emergency meetings, we discovered who the moneyed people in our congregation were and who we could go to in support of the synagogue. It was that information which helped us as we moved forward with some much -needed fund raising campaigns. Except for the initial sale of First Mortgage Bonds which enabled us to build the sanctuary, we had raised no significant money, either to pay off the debt incurred by those bonds or for the construction of the, now-in-progress, Rosenblum School Building.

For me it was also the beginning of my involvement with what was then UJA on the national scene and Federation on the local scene. The two national movements (UJA and the Council of Welfare Federations) ultimately merged into what became the United Jewish Community (UJC) and more recently the Jewish Federations of North America (JFNA) which raises money for local needs, Israel and distressed Jewish communities throughout the world. Slowly I began to understand the intricacies of the organized Jewish community which was determined to never again be less than completely prepared to address the ongoing challenges facing Jews both here and abroad as had tragically been the case before and deering World War II.

My years of service on the board of the Greater Miami Jewish Federation were very meaningful. I learned that others shared my passion for Jewish life and were willing to back up their feelings with significant offerings of both time and money. Initially I served on the Federation board by virtue of my position as president of the Rabbinic Association of Greater Miami, a role I was to fill on more than one occasion. Later I became the first Miami rabbi to be elected to the board in his own right- a source of considerable pride. From there it was a short step to the National Rabbinic Cabinet of the United Jewish Appeal where I learned that rabbis were taken much more seriously and could speak with far greater authority when they led not only with words but by example.

To be invited to become part of the Rabbinic Cabinet of UJA required that one make a minimum gift of $1000 to one's local campaign which was at first a stretch for me. But as the years went by, not only did giving $1000 (more in later years) became easier but I realized that if one was to ask others for money, whether for the synagogue or for the larger Jewish community, it was necessary to make a meaningful gift yourself or one lacked credibility. It was in the context of the Rabbinic Cabinet, which was comprised of rabbis from all streams of Jewish life and where we solicited each other, that I learned that *tzedakah* was truly an act of *righteous giving* and where I also deepened my commitment to the broader Jewish community. What emerged was a wonderful feeling of mutual respect among the colleagues. We were united by our love for the Jewish people and the State of Israel, despite the fact that we came from many places, were of different ages and represented a wide variety of ideological backgrounds. The Rabbinic Cabinet was one of the few places in American Jewish life where Orthodox and non-Orthodox Rabbis could sit side by side in common cause and with a feeling of total respect. It was emblematic of *Klal Yisrael*, the conviction that all Jews are responsible for one another, and represented a model of unity and cooperation that I tried to replicate throughout my career, albeit without ever foregoing my own loyalty to Liberal Judaism. That was who I was. I could not be someone else.

In later years, especially when I served a second term as president of the Rabbinic Association of Greater Miami, my great disappointment, despite personal friendships with Orthodox rabbis, was that our local Rabbinic Association would not become a meeting place for rabbis of all types. Reform, Conservative and Reconstructionist rabbis were responsive but the Orthodox, some bound by rulings of their *Roshei Yeshevot,* the seminary heads from whom they earned *S'micha* (ordination), others fearful of the reactions of their more right wing congregants, never allowed themselves to become full partners in the work of our local organization of rabbis. It was not only their loss, but the Jewish

Community was the poorer for it as well. Colleagues tell me to *let it go*, but it will always be a source of sadness and, even though I know it is not my fault, causes me to feel a sense of failure.

The period after the *Yom Kippur* War was thus one of personal growth for me and for the Synagogue. Our membership grew as did our reputation as North Dade County's Reform Congregation, albeit one with a decidedly traditional flavor. The sanctuary was full on Friday nights with 350–400 people because our worship was joyful and the messages from the pulpit were relevant to what was happening in the Jewish world and the secular world as well. I saw it as my task not only to bring our prayers to life but to apply Jewish values to the world in which we lived. At one point, I wrote a brief, tongue in cheek, article to the National Jewish Post, a Cincinnati based national Jewish newspaper, complaining that we had too many people coming to services on Friday night, many of them guests who came for the *Oneg Shabbat* which followed after worship. We were the envy of the neighborhood.

Our sons always came to synagogue with their mother as did the children of our friends and after services we would all go to Howard Johnson's or some other ice cream parlor for a second *Oneg Shabbat*. When in later years attendance declined and the spiritual environment was no longer as vital, I would think back nostalgically to those times realizing that there are stages in our lives which simply pass away as we age and that to replicate them is not possible. I realize that the success of a congregation is closely tied to the kind of community one is able to create. That community is often a product of the rhythms of the life cycle that people are going through. We and our friends were all of an age and shared common experiences as our children grew up. We were in car pools together and went to each other's *Bar* and *Bat Mitzvah* celebrations. It was truly *a way of life*. The problem is that we don't fully realize it until it is gone.

Sabbath mornings, I should add were equally joyful. While, by the mid 1970s we had *Bnai Mitzvah* most Saturdays, I consciously sought to create an environment where *Shabbat* worship and Torah study were not overshadowed by the presence of the many guests who had come to see the young man or woman *perform*. I felt then and still believe that *Shabbat* worship is the reason one goes to Temple and that the *Bar* or *Bat Mitzvah* should fit into the pattern of the service, not the reverse where the service is an adjunct to the *Bar* or *Bat Mitzvah*. That has become something of a losing battle today, I fear, at least in Reform congregations, some of which don't even have Sabbath morning services if there is no *Bar/Bat Mitzvah*. Worse yet, people have taken to having their children called to the Torah on Saturday afternoon thus creating a special service for the sake of the *Bar/Bat Mitzvah* since most Reform congregations do not have a regular *Shabbat Mincha* service. What that does is essentially privatize the ceremony which was originally meant to introduce a young man or woman to the larger Jewish community at atime when that community was gathered for prayer, namely on Saturday morning. Change of course is inevitable for it is part of the very fabric of life. Still there is a part of me that wishes that certain things which worked so well could be frozen in time.

The trauma of the *Yom Kippur* War gave way to a much happier time as during *Hanukah* of that year we dedicated the newly completed Irvin and Fanny Rosenblum Synagogue School Building. The building was to house our synagogue school where Hebrew was taught mid-week and other Jewish studies on Sunday morning. It would also house the two classes of our newly- established Nursery school which could now vacate its makeshift classrooms in the social hall behind the sanctuary.

The Early Childhood Program, as it became known in future years, grew rapidly over the next several years and spawned a summer day camp program as well. The school and the camp attracted young families and provided a base for future temple membership. So rapid was the growth during those years that before too much time had passed, we would begin looking for a way to expand our property. It was clear that we needed more space to accommodate our youngest children who, by code, where forbidden to climb the stairs of the Rosenblum Building to the second floor even though there were empty classrooms there. This led, over the course of some years, to the purchase of land directly to the

South of our property and eventually the building of an early childhood building.

Clearly the time had come for some serious fundraising, not only to help us pay off the owners of the bonds which had helped us to build the sanctuary but to pay for the construction of the school building which exceeded the amount of the Rosenblum gift and also to prepare for future needs which our success had begun to dictate. It should come as no surprise therefore that there would be a number of fundraising campaigns during the latter part of the 1970s and into the 1980s as Temple Sinai grew from the 150 families that greeted me in 1967 to the more than 700 families that were part of the synagogue I left to my successor when I retired in 1998. Fortunately, because of the confluence of time and events and enhanced by our cutting edge approach to Reform Judaism, we were able to attract people who identified with what we were trying to achieve and who were willing to help. This is not the place to list them but they are acknowledged by name on buildings and plaques throughout the Temple Sinai campus. They made my journey much easier. That journey, however, took yet another turn in 1981. That was the year we launched the Sinai Academy (to become the Jacobson Sinai Academy), a Liberal Jewish day school.

A NEW DIMENSION

Martin Luther King was not the only one to have had a dream. During the early years of my rabbinate at Temple Sinai, I came to the realization that no matter how good our synagogue schools might be, the Jewish education they provided was still, at best, part time and thus very limited. There was just so much a young boy or girl could learn during two hours on Sunday morning and another two hours during the week, which they would come to after a tiring day at their various secular schools. We were after all trying to teach something of the grandeur of a people's 3,000 year history together with its language, its holy books and customs and ceremonies, even as we sought to impart the importance of its unique ethics and values. All of that while making it a fun experience so that the children would want to come back. We tried our best, but it was an impossible task.

Traditional Judaism understood the challenge and sidestepped it by establishing a network of Jewish day schools which were in place of public schools. Children would be taught the necessary secular subjects for half a day but be engaged in Jewish studies for the other half, not for several hours per week but on a daily basis. The education began at home, of course, but then continued in pre-school and from there, went through elementary and into high school. The result was a cadre of seriously educated young Jews. At the same time, the children were, of course, also indoctrinated into the ways of Orthodox (or in some cases, Conservative) Judaism and entered college and the adult world with Jewish religious commitment that went far beyond that of the average Jewish young person who was not reared in that kind of environment.

Reform Judaism, historically grounded in the notion that the public school system was central to the American way of life feared that any kind of parochial school education would weaken the public schools and was on record as being opposed to parochial schools, whether Catholic or Jewish. Sectarian schools seemed at odds with the uniquely American notion of the melting pot which saw the coming together of children of different backgrounds as ultimately strengthening our way of life. Jews, of all people, having come from places where they were forced to be separated from those in whose midst they lived, were now at last able to be integrated into the larger society, and should therefore embrace that opportunity, not move away from it. So went the argument and I, a product of such thinking, well understood the logic and for the early part of my rabbinate, totally agreed with it.

But times were changing. Some voices in the Liberal Jewish community began to question the common wisdom set forth above. They understood the shortcomings of part time Jewish education. They recognized that given the Holocaust, which saw the slaughter of six million Jews (one-and-a-half million of them children who never got the chance to go to any kind of school), and as a result of the Six Days War when Jewish existence again was threatened, we needed to revise our thinking. We needed to put our own existential needs before ideological considerations. The present need was clearly for the creation of a generation of educated and committed Jews who would be the leaders of our people during the next period of time.

It was against that background and not without a good deal of controversy that some communities and a handful of individual congregations began to explore the possibility of creating a Liberal Jewish day school. As in other matters described above, Rabbi Herbert Baumgard was among the pioneers. He created one of the first such schools at his synagogue in Kendall, Temple Beth Am. I resolved one day to follow suit but not until I had gone down a different path.

As I pointed out earlier, my Jewish journey had led me to embrace a view of Judaism which was grounded in the somewhat idealistic thought that Jews of differing theological commitments could come together and while remaining true to their own ideologies, find a way to function side by side in common cause, each respecting the other irrespective of differences. It worked to an extent in the Federation world and in such venues as the Rabbinic Cabinet of UJA and at times in local rabbinic bodies. Why could it not work in a Jewish day school? That was my hope as a group of us gathered in North Miami Beach and talked about starting a community day school that would be identified with no particular stream of Judaism but would be a place where children from Orthodox, Conservative, Reform and even secularist Jewish homes could come together to learn. It would mean that children would be exposed to differing points of view represented by teachers from the Traditional as well as the Liberal world and could find a space that would be comfortable for them without the implication that there was only one right way to be Jewish. The idea was that it would be a true community school in terms of faculty as well as student body.

I still believe very strongly that such a school can exist and be a model for us all to embrace. But after many meetings it became clear that it was an idea whose time had not yet come. A day school did come to pass in North Dade County not far from Temple Sinai, but while it is, to this day, called The Hillel Jewish Community Day School, it is Orthodox all but in name and leaves no room for any ideology other than Orthodoxy. While there are many reasons for this having happened, the fact is that those who were rooted in an Orthodox background won the day and were willing to back up their commitment with the necessary start-up funds. There were also people who, while themselves not Orthodox in their personal practices, came from more traditional backgrounds and neither understood nor were sympathetic to a more Liberal framework which allows for a greater diversity of Jewish expressions. It was an opportunity missed.

Our older son Evan Moshe actually attended Hillel during the first two years of the school's existence, and Jonathan Meir ,our younger son, also attended for several years at a later time. They both gained much by way of Jewish knowledge but it was clear that children from Liberal Jewish homes like our sons were made to feel that their brand of Judaism was inferior to that of the prevailing Orthodoxy. I did not need to hear such talk from my children, nor did the parents of other neighborhood children who attended the school but were members of a Reform or Conservative synagogue. Ironically some of the early supporters of the Hillel School were affiliated with Conservative congregations and seemed untroubled, even pleased, by the turn of events. But for me, the time was ripe to explore other options.

Could Temple Sinai perhaps establish its own day school in which Jewish values would pervade an integrated curriculum throughout the day in a Liberal as opposed to an Orthodox environment? In which Hebrew as the spoken language of the Jewish people would be taught together with other Jewish subjects as well as the normal fare of any Elementary School? It would be a challenge but there were those in our synagogue who shared that vision and who were willing to work for its realization with me.

We would not be the first to have pursued such a goal, nor would we be entirely alone and without examples to follow. While few in number, several Liberal Jewish day schools did exist having been established in the United States and in Canada. Some were community based and some, like the Temple Beth Am day school referred to above, were connected to a synagogue. The time was ripe. So we began to dream and to plan.

Much went into the process. We clearly had the space. The Rosenblum Building housed the rapidly growing early childhood program but there were empty classrooms that were used only for mid- week Hebrew classes and Sunday School and could easily be adapted for use as day school spaces. We needed to formalize a philosophy which would provide a framework for the learning that was to take place and to develop a curriculum. We needed to engage teachers who were Jewishly knowledgeable yet comfortable in a non- Orthodox setting; who could teach both secular as well as Jewish subjects.

One of our convictions was that we ought not have an environment that was secular for half a day and Jewish for the other half but rather where the two halves became one integrated whole. Apart from being educationally sound, such an approach would set us apart from more traditional Jewish day schools. We also needed to find a director who had both the educational and the Jewish credentials to help us put the pieces together. As well, before proceeding, we needed to convince the Board of Trustees that our project would not become a burden to the synagogue; that it would in fact benefit both the synagogue and the Jewish community; that it would strengthen our Jewish future. And not least of all, we needed a means to pay for it all.

None of that was easy and took us more than a few years to accomplish. But in the end, the Sinai Academy opened its doors in the fall of 1981 with eighteen children divided into a Kindergarten and a combined First and Second Grade. From there we grew slowly and deliberately, picking up additional students and adding another grade each year until we had six grades with double classes at the lower levels. Before we knew it, we had our first graduation in 1986 as fourteen students completed the sixth grade. I spoke to the graduates about their memories but said: *Wonderful as they are, it is not the memories of yesterday that count but what we do with our tomorrows.*

I didn't know it then but our tomorrows came just a few years later, when Dade County announced its intention to convert to a K-5 elementary and 6-8 middle school structure. So we began to explore the possibility of adding a seventh and eighth grade. Not to have done so would have meant dropping our sixth grade, a backward step in the eyes of many of us. After a number of surveys which didn't provide much new information not already known to us, much soul searching, and a large measure of faith such as that which we had relied on before, we moved forward much in the manner of Nachshon ben Amminadab who led the Israelites into the foreboding waters of the Sea of Reeds. It was only when he showed the courage to move ahead, that the people followed and the waters parted. So had it been with us when we started the Sinai Academy. So was it in 1998 when we began the Middle School helped by leadership gifts from the Stuart (Cindy) Israelson and George (Marla) Bergmann families. We had the courage and the faith to move ahead.

That faith, all along, resided in a group of dedicated lay people, willing partners who believed in our project through the years and who were willing and anxious to enroll their children, at first as pioneer students, and later as anxious and happy learners. It was given expression especially during the challenging beginning times by the efforts of Rabbi Julian Cook, whom I brought to Temple Sinai as my associate rabbi for education and youth in 1978 for the precise purpose of helping me birth our school. He had been at Temple Beth Am where he served as Herbert Baumgard's education rabbi. While he was not responsible for the Beth Am Day School, he was familiar with its workings firsthand and could apply the lessons he learned to our exciting new venture. He became the architect of our experiment. Though our parting ten years later, a few years before the beginning of our middle school, was not under the best circumstances, I am forever indebted to him for those early years and their result which is that the Jacobson Sinai Academy, as it is now known, with its Bergmann Upper School, today educates upwards of 400 children from early childhood through eighth grade and is a highly respected institution, not only in our local community but on the national scene. Its creation and success is one of the proudest achievements of my years at Temple Sinai and an important part of my journey.

While my sons were already in high school and college when the Sinai Academy opened its doors, my two local grandchildren, Julia and Max were both recipients of an Academy education, Julia through the fifth grade and Max through the second when both left for other educational opportunities. My regret is that they did not remain longer for studies have shown that Jewish learning experienced in the upper grades has a more lasting impact than that acquired in the elementary grades. That notwithstanding, what they learned in just those few years has remained with them and is evident whenever we come together for *Passover* or *Hanukah*. It totally validates my still strong conviction that Jewish day schools serve an invaluable function in raising levels of Jewish literacy and commitment.

The cost of day school education has risen dramatically since our beginning days making it difficult for all but the very wealthy to send their children. An influx of Jews from Latin America who are well to-do and are used to sending their children to private Jewish schools have helped to sustain the Jacobson Sinai Academy, so called as a result of a generous gift from Jeanette Jacobson. It continues to do well as I write these words. But I worry about what the future holds in store for Jewish day schools and for the families they are intended to serve who may no longer be able to afford them. At some point, the Jewish community is going to have to find a way to subsidize its schools and students far more generously than they do now if we are to produce the next generation of Jewishly literate and committed young people who will be our leaders tomorrow. Full time Jewish education must not be a luxury item for the rich. Together with Jewish camps and trips to Israel, day schools are a necessity for us all if we are to insure a meaningful Jewish future and should become a number one priority for those who raise funds for Jewish causes.

IT'S EXPENSIVE TO BE A JEW

B ut my journey took me elsewhere in the 1980s as well. The rabbis, after all had long ago taught us *ein kemach, ein Torah,* that without flour (for bread) there can be no Torah (learning). So the task of raising funds for much-needed physical expansion became a major preoccupation even as spiritual growth had been the focus during my earlier Sinai years. Out of necessity more than choice, I became a fund raiser. Fortunately there were those who responded to my entreaties for money even as they had responded earlier to my entreaties for heightened Jewish observance.

As a result, we were able to buy adjacent land which had become available and to build more buildings to accommodate our growing congregation and especially the increasing number of young children who were entrusted to us by their parents, and for whom we needed more classroom space. A new early childhood building bearing their name was made possible by the generosity of a devoted couple from Chicago, Arnold and Roselyn Meyer. A building to house additional classrooms for older children, a chapel, to provide a more intimate praying space than the large sanctuary for our older students as well as adults, and an already existing library became a reality thanks to a major gift by Connie and Herb Weinberg after whom that structure was named. The chapel was given in memory of her parents by Caroline Kemelhor. The library recalls a gift by one of our founding families, the Hollanders and their children, the Rachleffs. There was also a major gift from the Feinbloom family from Rochester after whom the sanctuary was named. All became part of what, together with the earlier buildings is now known as the Kemelhor Campus.

While there are many who over the years played an important role in my spiritual journey, many more than I have named, one, in this context of building, is especially worthy of mention. Ironically, he is probably the last to have wanted to bring attention to himself. He never asked for nor did he expect anything in return for all that he did. Yet without him, I wonder if Temple Sinai would have become the important institution that it became. His name was George Berlin. He is the same George Berlin who is responsible for so much of what evolved from a country club surrounded by a few high rise buildings called Turnberry Isle, in the early 1970s, into the City of Aventura which, not without reason, calls itself The City of Excellence.

He was an extraordinary man who saved us countless sums in construction costs by himself serving as our general contractor or by having one of his employees at Turnberry do so and, by having his sub contractors do work for us at no cost or very low cost. At the same time, he rarely missed a Sabbath Eve Service and he loved Temple Sinai with a special love. He and his wife Lila are today memorialized by a Bridge which connects our Temple Sinai Campus to the Michael-Ann Russell JCC, the fulfillment of a long held dream. Sadly, he never lived to see it come to pass but as long as both institutions thrive, his memory will live on.

While fund raising was not part of the curriculum at HUC-JIR, and while it may not seem to be part of a spiritual journey, in point of fact, I learned that both the act of asking for money to support a noble cause and the act of giving can also become holy acts. Accordingly, I was able to help teach those who were privileged with the blessing of plenty that it is their obligation to support worthy purposes, whether to feed the hungry and to clothe the naked, as the Prophets of old urged or, in the case of synagogue life, to make it possible for our young to get a Torah education. Overwhelmingly, those in our congregation who were so blessed understood that obligation, and we who did the asking understood that we were helping them to perform a *mitzvah*. And both of us were the more fulfilled as a result.

That was a lesson I tried to teach our *Bnai Mitzvah* and their parents when I met with them several weeks before their big day. Patiently I explained to our soon- to- be thirteen year olds that they would be on the receiving end of many gifts, a significant number of them in cash. How they used those gifts would be one way of demonstrating how much they learned from the experience. I suggested that they take a small portion of what they would receive, say $100, and use it to support Jewish life by making a gift to the Greater Miami Jewish Federation or by purchasing an Israel Bond. Virtually all of them complied and got started on the road to *tzedakah*. I would also suggest to the parents that it was appropriate to include the synagogue in their giving at a time when they had much to be thankful for, and also to symbolically invite the less fortunate to their parties by donating 3% of their party expenses to Mazon, an organization devoted to feeding the hungry. Happily, most did. Of course, the synagogue benefitted but the family felt good as well. To be sure, it is expensive to be a Jew. But it can be enormously rewarding.

LET MY PEOPLE GO

B ut there were also many social issues looming large on the Jewish horizon during those years which had nothing to do with money, at least not directly. In the 1970s and well into the 1980s, the plight of Soviet Jewry became a major concern of mine and that of a number of caring congregants as well. I had actually begun to pay attention to what was happening to the Jews of Russia as early as the late 1950s when I attended a Social Action Conference in Atlantic City and heard Rabbi George Lieberman, in whose synagogue in Rockville Center Brenda and I were to be married, speak about the *Jews of Silence* and the *Anatomy of Fear* which pervaded the lives of the Jews of Russia. They could not freely attend synagogue, were not permitted to study or teach Hebrew or to live outwardly Jewish lives. Nor were they allowed to emigrate and to go to places like Israel, which was ready to welcome them with open arms. Rabbi Lieberman told of an elderly Jew with whom he sat on a bench and chatted in Yiddish whose parting words, spoken softly for fear that he might be watched, were *Vergisst uns nisht- Don't forget us.*

I was very moved by that experience so when the opportunity arose some years later while I was in Garden City, I organized an interfaith rally on behalf of Soviet Jewry which was held in the Episcopal Cathedral with the full cooperation of its cannon, Dean Harold Lemoine and had the support of our local congressman, John Wydler, as well. To say that Garden City was not known for its open-armed welcome of Jews is an understatement. But somehow, this was a cause that captured the imagination of even those crusty upper middle class gentiles who added their voices to those of the Jewish community and engaged in a letter writing campaign which urged the Soviet government to *Let My People Go.*

It was natural therefore, some years later, by which time the Soviet Jewry movement had begun to take on a life of its own, for us at Temple Sinai to become a center for local Soviet Jewry activities. I'm proud to say that much of the leadership of what became the South Florida Conference of Soviet Jewry came out of our synagogue and helped, through their actions, to write one of the proudest chapters of American Jewish history. Ours was certainly not the only synagogue involved, but we were there at the beginning and until that wonderful day in 1989 when the Berlin Wall came down and the Jews of Russia could finally be open about their Judaism without fear of persecution.

Several years after we had arrived in North Miami Beach, Brenda, I and our two small boys found ourselves on a bus filled with activists heading to Cape Canaveral, site of what was to be called The Kennedy Space Center, where we participated in a rally on behalf of Soviet Jewry timed to coincide with the launching of a space craft. We had spent many hours on the floor of our Social Hall coloring in Save Soviet Jewry posters which we held up in clear sight of the media who had been alerted to our effort.

As we witnessed an increasing number of Soviet Jews being harassed and even imprisoned for attempting to exercise what we in the USA take so much for granted- freedom of speech and the right to openly practice our religion, each in our own way- our focus was to make their plight known. Thus, we pressured our own government to place human rights on the agenda of all international meetings and to create linkages when considering economic agreements by means of which benefits to the Soviets would be dependent on how they treated their Jewish population. The best known and, some think, most effective of those linkages was the Jackson-Vannick Amendment. It made the much coveted *Favored Nation Status* which offered certain economic advantages, dependent on how the Soviet Union treated its Jews. The American Secretary of State, Henry Kissinger (my distant cousin) was opposed to its passage but it was one of those times that history proved his *Real Politik* wrong.

At the same time, we reached out to make contact with those who had become known as *Prisoners of Conscience*, the most famous of whom was Natan (then Anatoly) Sharansky. The *crime*, for which he was jailed, along with other like-minded Russian Jews, was that he wanted to live a Jewish life and have the right to leave the Soviet Union and go to Israel with his new wife Avital. We wrote letters, we made phone calls and created a program whereby each Bar and Bat Mitzvah boy and girl was twinned with a Russian thirteen-year-old who was not permitted by Soviet Law to celebrate his or her coming to the Age of Commandments. Many wrote letters to their *twins* and some lucky few actually received answers. In addition, each *Bar* and *Bat Mitzvah* received a large Jewish Star containing the name of one of the Prisoners of Conscience about whom we spoke on the morning of their big day. The plight of Soviet Jewry was thus kept before all who worshipped with us on Sabbath after Sabbath. As a footnote to that extraordinary twinning program, my son Evan was one of the lucky ones to receive an answer from his twin, Misha Taratuta. Magically, after many years, they met in NYC and are still in touch to this very day.

But perhaps the most meaningful action that was undertaken on behalf of Soviet Jewry was the visits. At the behest of, and with the financial and logistic help of the State of Israel, the two major national Soviet Jewry organizations, the National Conference on Soviet Jewry (NCSJ) and the Union of Councils for Soviet Jewry (UCSJ), arranged for hundreds of trips to visit *refuseniks* by rabbis and laypeople who were committed to the cause. NCJS was part of the Federation establishment and the UCSJ, a grassroots movement. But the two organizations, while sometimes at odds with one another as to strategy, worked towards the same goal: to *Let My People Go*.

The trips had both a spiritual and a material purpose. Spiritually, those who visited were living examples that we American Jews cared and that those brave souls who were taking great risks to cling to their Jewish faith were not forgotten; that we were working hard to help them attain freedom and to live Jewish lives, whether in the United States or in Israel. Thus each visitor brought hope to those extraordinarily brave people.

But the trips also had a material purpose. Each visitor snuck in a variety of life-saving items whether badly needed medicines or such things as American jeans, cameras, or radios, that could be sold on the black market for valuable rubles which in turn, could then be used to buy the necessities of every- day living. Equally important, the visitors brought Jewish books and ritual items such as *tefilin* and *talitot* which were not available or even illegal in the Soviet Union.

It is such a mission that I undertook with a colleague, the late Rabbi Jeffrey Ballon, in 1984, at a time when things were not going well for the Jews of Russia. As chair of the Soviet Jewry Committee of my national rabbinic body, the Central Conference of American Rabbis (CCAR), I had been asked to sit on the board of the NCSJ. I therefore had an insider's view of what was happening in the USSR- the daily harassments often leading to arrests and in some cases jail sentences, the anatomy of fear and intimidation and of course, the ongoing refusal to allow Jewish learning, not to speak of permission to emigrate. In addition, I was in constant contact with local Soviet Jewry activists who kept me well informed as to what was happening within the Russian Jewish community on an almost daily basis. Thus, when I was invited to undertake my "mission," it did not take long for me to say yes.

Each trip was well-planned and those of us who travelled to visit *refuseniks* began to prepare long before we left- in my case, in the late spring for a September departure. Not only did we need to become familiar with the people whom we were assigned to visit and their stories, but we needed to learn the dos and don'ts of acting as tourists. We were, of course, not ordinary tourists. We needed to know how to behave and what to do remembering that what we did was not without danger. We committed as much as we could to memory and devised ways of coding names and places so that in case we were stopped and searched, we would not endanger others not to speak of ourselves. It was helpful to familiarize ourselves with the Russian Cyrillic alphabet so that we would be able at least to read street signs and recognize subway stops. It was not thought advisable to travel by cab since tourists were supposed to be with their tour guides and not on their own. Remember, the USSR in those days was a totalitarian country and we were going on what was akin to a spy mission. We spent the summer months preparing and by September 2, Jeffrey and I were ready and made our way to JFK Airport from which we departed on our adventure to the USSR.

We were something of an odd couple. Jeffrey, was ten years my junior. I knew him since my growing up years in Long Island where his father Sydney was a beloved Rabbi in nearby West Hempstead. He was a free spirit although he was extremely bright and, unlike me, had a phenomenal memory so that he could easily remember names and places. Together we ventured forth on our mission, making our visits in Moscow and Leningrad, and delivering the books, medicines, jeans and electronic gadgets we were given to bring with us. Most of all, we tried to bring encouragement and hope, and wherever possible, we did, as the old joke has it, *a little teaching on the side,* usually about Jewish life in America and about Reform Judaism in particular about which not much was known. Thus we spent four days in Moscow and four in Leningrad (today, St. Petersburg). It was all very emotional and all enormously gratifying.

Mainly, we travelled by subway and by foot as per our instructions. But one night in Leningrad, we went against the rules and allowed ourselves to be driven back to our hotel in a private car, something tourists were forbidden to do. But Michael M., whom we had met in the synagogue that morning and with whom we had visited (also against the rules for he was not on the approved list of those we were assigned to see) insisted. Along with his adorable six year old daughter, he proceeded to drive us back to our hotel at the end of a delightful evening of food, drink and conversation. Everything was pleasant as we chatted and sang Hebrew songs along the way; everything, until the police drove up behind us and stopped Michael for speeding. Surely we would be thrown in jail, we thought. Who would know what happened to us? We feared the worst. But fortunately, after several harrowing minutes during which Jeffrey and I sat in frightened silence holding each other's hand, we were simply placed into a cab and driven the rest of the way to our hotel, while Michael and his daughter had to make their way back home without their car. The police remove the license plate when one is stopped for a traffic violation. They do not fool around.

That was the atmosphere in Russia. At worst we came to experience, at first hand, the oppressive environment about which we had read and been briefed: the need to whisper in our hotel rooms for fear that our rooms were bugged and that our conversations might be recorded; the requirement to report to the key lady at the head of each floor with whom we left our keys so she could keep tabs on our comings and goings; always looking over our shoulder to make sure we weren't being followed or spied upon. On a lesser level, we had to learn to put up with daily inconveniences such as not being served coffee with our meals for there was none.

But, unlike the people with whom we visited and the several million other Jews who lived in that oppressive environment every day, we could leave and return to our Jewish schools and synagogues and to the freedoms we take so for granted. We did not have to practice our Judaism in secret but could publically celebrate the cycle of our years. They, on the other hand, who could not give expression to or learn about their Jewish heritage except in secret, if at all, lived with the constant knowledge that they might go to jail if they made a wrong move. We were saddened and troubled by what we saw during our all too brief eight days. But we were also enormously heartened by the great courage and the undying spirit of those with whom we met and came away even more determined than before to help work for their freedom.

A detailed record titled My Trip to Russia is on file in the archives of the American Jewish Historical Society for anyone who wishes more details. It is important for me to say that I consider it one of the most important by-ways of my spiritual journey. Whatever our presence did for those Jews whom we met, they did every bit as much and considerably more for the two of us. Those brave souls with whom we interacted demonstrated in a most dramatic way why we are an undying people who, in every generation, have found a way to say no to adversity and yes to life. The cost has been great, but like the biblical Jacob, also called Israel, we have wrestled with the angel and prevailed.

Our efforts, which, in addition to all I have described above, included my having been arrested for demonstrating in front of the Soviet Embassy with a group of rabbis and Soviet Jewry activists and spending several hours in jail (not a fun experience), were rewarded when the Russian government began finally to give permission for numbers of Jewish families to leave. Many went to Israel but others chose to come to the United States. Again, our synagogue, with the help of the South Florida Conference for Soviet Jewry swung into action. We were able to rent and furnish apartments for several families whom we sponsored when they came to our shores, and saw them through their first months until they were able to manage on their own. It was so gratifying to see them learn English and to discover their Jewish identity as members of our congregation. For the first time, they discovered what it meant to belong to a synagogue and took delight as their children began to receive a Jewish education having been enrolled in our day school at no expense to them. We for our part discovered the deeper meaning of our own Jewish identity as we were able to fulfill the oft-repeated biblical admonition to bring freedom to the captive and to welcome the stranger in our midst. Our Jewish values really came alive.

MORE ON JEWISH VALUES AT WORK

It was precisely those Jewish values as I understood them that drove much of my rabbinate and moved me along my spiritual path. They spoke to me and motivated me as I read the words of the prayer book and taught Torah each Friday night and Shabbat morning. They informed my teaching and my preaching and I hope, also the way I conducted myself and lived my life. Thus, I spoke out against our involvement in Vietnam because I could not reconcile the death and destruction caused by what seemed so clearly to be an unjust war with the fact that the Torah's *paths are peace*. Closer to home I could not be silent, even though it upset some of my congregants, when efforts to integrate our public schools and to enable black children to receive the same educational benefits as whites were being frustrated by otherwise good people who were against segregation and okay with attempts to achieve integration until it came to their own neighborhood.

A particular issue in the early 1970's that turned particularly nasty involved Dade County's attempt to bus children from schools with largely black populations to schools that were predominantly white. In return, a like number of white children were to be bused to predominantly black schools thus creating a more appropriate racial mix reflective of the community beyond the neighborhood. The grades chosen for what seemed to me to be a fair way to achieve integration that would ultimately benefit both black and white children, even on a very minimal level, were grades one and six. My younger son Jonathan would have been among those bused. At a PTA meeting where the suggestion was discussed, I spoke in its favor and pleaded with those assembled not to become *a bunch of Jewish Archie Bunkers* in their opposition.

In retrospect, while my intentions were good, and my understanding of the Jewish ethical imperative clear, the allusion to the popular TV show about an entertaining but clearly bigoted central character was ill chosen, to say the least. It actually led to threats against me and my family. I had failed to understand the strong opposition by parents who feared for the safety of their children more than they were concerned about the inferior education received by children of black families who lived in less affluent and influential neighborhoods than their own. The plain truth was that the phrase which appears more often than any other in the Torah-*Remember the stranger for you were strangers in the land of Egypt*-did not trump the instincts of Jewish parenthood and included not only keeping their children from harm's way, but a strong commitment to their receiving the best possible education. Both, they feared, would be compromised by busing.

They were, of course, not entirely wrong. I personally learned that competing values sometimes make it hard for even well intentioned people to find good answers to thorny problems. With sadness, I must admit that while there can be no doubt that we have made significant progress, and while the specific issue faded away because the school board eventually withdrew their proposal, the problem of black-white Integration or lack thereof still exists in the United States, some of it structural, some of it, self imposed. This is not the place to pontificate except to remind those who read these words of what Rabbi Tarphon taught long ago: *(While) it is not incumbent on you to finish the task, you are not free to desist from it.* So I still try to stay engaged if no more than to be a voice of conscience albeit, hopefully, with a bit more political savvy then I displayed in those earlier days.

THE GAY REVOLUTION

It was with that voice of conscience that I also tried to make our synagogue a place in which gay and lesbian people (Transgender was not yet a commonly used term) could feel at home and be accepted long before any straight people, myself included, ever dreamt that someday there would be such a thing as gay marriage. To have done less would have been to ignore the words of the prophet Amos: *Have we not all one Father? Has not one God created us?* My attitude about gay rights was itself something of a journey which began in 1977 when Anita Bryant, then a popular star and spokeswoman for Tropicana orange juice began a crusade against a Dade County Gay Rights Ordinance which prohibited discrimination for reasons of sexual orientation. I preached my first sermon on the subject of Gay Rights on Jan. 28th of that year titled: *The Gay Lifestyle and Society-Whose Problem Is It? Or, Why Is Anita Bryant So Uptight?* In it I strongly objected to the attempt to repeal what I viewed as a perfectly proper Human Rights Ordinance. I viewed gay rights purely through the lens of the civil rights movement. Gays were no less entitled to equal protection from being discriminated against then were blacks or women. What I had no appreciation for in those days was what was going on in the heart and soul of the GLBT population. It would take a while for me to begin to understand just what it was that made them who they were.

Sixteen years later, in the presence of our then gay neighbor, Congregation Eytz Chaim, whom we had invited to worship with us, I reflected on the evolution of my views and admitted that in those days (1978), I did not know much about the gay psyche. Even though I believed gay people needed to have the full protection of the Law and be protected from discrimination, I looked upon the gay life style as a form of deviant behavior not particularly acceptable within a Jewish framework which stressed marriage, children and continuity. But by 1993, my views had evolved not only as a result of my reading but, more significantly, as a result of personal encounters with gay Jewish men and women some of whom had been my *Bar* and *Bat Mitzvah* students and others who had come for counseling. They explained that they had not chosen to be gay. It was how they were born. It was who they were. They knew they were different from early childhood on and shared their pain at needing to live lives of deceit, afraid that they would be *outed* to their employers or their parents. I still have letters in my file, written anonymously during those less enlightened days, for fear that their secret might become known.

As more time passed I have come to know gay colleagues who are good rabbis and the parents of gay sons and daughters in need of support. I came to realize that if being gay is not a matter of choice but a chance event of birth, it is our duty not only to insure that gay persons are protected under the law but that our own attitudes reflect that reality. I have come to believe that gay and lesbian persons are entitled to every human benefit that is available to straight people including also the right to marry and to raise a family with the person they love. How ironic that the Christian Right that decries the breakdown of marriage will not support efforts by loving people who happen to be of the same sex to establish lasting relationships with each other which can only strengthen the institution of marriage. How can we offer them less? Happily, since a Supreme Court ruling on June 26, 2015, same-sex marrage is now the law of the land and therefore legal in all states. Just in the few years since I began to write these words, there has been a veritable revolution in the thinking of Middle America. It is one of the amazing happenings of this era, and I am proud to be on the right side of history.

GOING BACK TO SCHOOL

As the years passed, my journey took yet another small detour. At Brenda's suggestion, I enrolled in a degree program at St. Thomas, a small Catholic University in Miami Gardens, and began to work towards a master's degree in family therapy. As a rabbi, I had been practicing family therapy of sorts all along but without any formal background except for a few courses in human relations during seminary days. Now as the rather new field was beginning to gain acceptability as a legitimate approach to counseling (it began as a discipline with its own name in the 1970's), I took the opportunity while working towards a second master's degree not only to expand my knowledge base (always a worthy goal), but also to acquire some practical skills that would help me be a better rabbi during my remaining active years. At the back of my mind, was also the thought that I might someday (I was 53 at the time) have another profession to pursue in retirement, if I so desired. While no specific time for my retirement had yet been established, it turned out to be only eleven years away when I began my two year course of night classes in 1987.

Apart from the academic challenge, my time at St. Thomas was a further growth experience on many levels. Most dramatically, it exposed me to a universe of discourse that was entirely new. As a rabbi, my approach had been to be an enabler and a fixer: to help people who came to me with a problem or who were in search to find a solution by injecting myself and my expertise, such as it was, into the situation. With Jewish values as my frame of reference, my role was frequently to make judgments about who or what was right or wrong. In brief, to give advice about how to handle a particular issue. As a therapist, I had to learn how to help people find their own solutions. I could not be judgmental but instead had to motivate those who sought my help to gain insight without favoring one person or one view over another or injecting my own opinion. The wise rabbinic counselor is the one who can wear his or her rabbinic hat and therapist's hat at the same time, not always an easy or advisable task. We were taught during our seminary years to be careful not to confuse roles but rather to refer congregants to mental health professionals before becoming too deeply involved in counseling situations which might well be beyond our area of expertise.

That universe of discourse was new also in the respect that it taught us to focus not so much on the individual and his or her concerns but to see that individual in the context of a family unit. That is the difference between family therapy and more traditional psychotherapy. The latter focuses on the person seeking counseling, his or her background, sometimes going back many years in time, and whatever issues are relevant to that person as an individual. The former focuses on the larger family unit. Thus, instead of seeing only the identified patient, for example, a problem child, a family therapist might ask the mother, father and siblings to come along to therapy as well and would deal with them together, at least some of the time. The family therapist might do the same with a person having marital problems, seeing him or her together with his or her spouse rather than working with the husband or wife alone. In truth, none of us exists in a vacuum. We are all formed by and respond to, for better or worse, all the influences upon us. We are part of a social system that functions organically and so need to be understood within that context even as an electron needs to be seen in its field. That does not mean that we do not bear ultimate responsibility for who we are and what we do for each of us has free will and can choose the path we follow. But certainly, our persona is best understood as part of a larger system, a *gestalt*.

Perhaps the most dramatic revelation of those two years was that there existed a world of which I was blissfully and naively unaware and had been sheltered from by dint of good fortune. So many of my classmates during those two years at St. Thomas University had come from broken homes or had been abused by alcoholic or addicted parents or were themselves recovering alcoholics or addicts. Maybe that is why they were attracted to a healing profession; they wanted to help others who, like themselves, had been through traumatic times. I came to recognize how fortunate I had been in my own upbringing and how blessed my home and family was, in contrast to the many people who suffer in ways that are often unfathomable. And if I didn't realize it before, I also came to see how great the human spirit is in its ability to overcome adversity, even under the most unimaginable circumstances.

While I did earn my Master of Science in Family Therapy, thoroughly enjoying the process which included some hours of internship in mental health facilities during the final semesters, I never did pursue family therapy as a new career. To have become a licensed family therapist, I would have had to log several thousand hours in practice, something that would have conflicted with my day job for I still had to shepherd my flock at Temple Sinai. Moreover, I understood that one could not be a therapist half-heartedly. As I needed to be available to my congregants, so I would need to be available to my clients. And thinking ahead to retirement, which was all about not being tied down to a schedule, I understood that I could not tell a client in need that I would be back in the office in several weeks or a month because I would be away on a trip. I was not willing to surrender the freedom retirement was to bring. That having been said, I did gain much from the experience by way of knowledge and insight which I hope helped me to become a better rabbi during my last years in the active rabbinate and a wiser, more sensitive human being as well.

BY-PATHS ALONG THE JOURNEY

L est I give the impression that my journey was all work and no play, I should point out that frequently the two intersected. That is, even as I was working, there was time for play as well. I was fortunate over the years to have been able to do a good bit of travelling on my way to and from my annual rabbinical convention (Central Conference of American Rabbis) and the biennial conventions of the Union of American Hebrew Congregations (now the Union for Reform Judaism). Those conventions which were times for learning as well as for socializing were always held in major cities around the country so Brenda, who usually accompanied me, and I got to see a good deal of the United States over the years. They were inevitably times for recharging my spiritual batteries. I always came home enthused having learned new program ideas and having experienced a sense of being part of something larger than my own community, wonderful as it may have been.

The most inspiring and enriching of those times were those that took me to Israel which, despite the fact that I had grown up without any real Zionist indoctrination, were like a homecoming. I came to understand the words of the great Spanish poet Judah HaLevi who famously wrote, *I am in the West but my heart is in the East.* According to legend, he was killed by an Arab just as he came upon Jerusalem after years of yearning, a tragic and premature end to his life just as his dream was about to be fulfilled. I was more fortunate. I came alive in a new way after my first visit to Israel in 1970, not long after the Six Days War when there was still something wonderfully pristine and idealistic about that amazing land. I was overwhelmed by the sense of history, every stone having a story to tell, and by the people we met, so filled with hope about the future despite being surrounded by hostile neighbors and having already known years of war and conflict. Moreover, they were still living within the shadow of the Holocaust which took six million of our people, 1.5 million of them children who were never to know the promise of their tomorrow. Israel spoke to my Jewish soul in a way nothing else had until that time.

The occasion for what was to be the first of many visits was the annual convention of our Reform rabbinic body, the Central Conference of American Rabbis, to which I alluded earlier, held for the first time in Jerusalem. To understand the revolutionary nature of that event, one has to understand that the Reform movement, was historically anti-Zionist and then, at best, non-Zionist into the 1940s. The anti-Zionist American Council for Judaism, with some significant support from Reform rabbis and laymen who rejected the concept of a Jewish state, had after all, been established as late as 1942.

All of that began to slowly change, however, after World War II and especially after 1948 when the modern state became an existential reality. One life-long anti-Zionist Rabbi captured the evolving mood when he renounced his long-held position saying *either we are for the Jewish People or we are against them*, in a pulpit oration. The Six Days War in 1967, when we realized that not only Israel but the entire world Jewish population was threatened as Israel stood alone while the attempt was made to eliminate her from among the family of nations, forever changed the minds of all but the intransigent few and made Zionists of us all.

While each of my many trips to Israel was exciting in its own way, whether with a group from the Temple (I believe Brenda and I led ten or twelve congregational trips over the years) or on a mission with UJA, Israel Bonds or the Greater Miami Jewish Federation, the first was the most magical. I gave expression to my excitement in the journal I kept (as I did for each of my trips) noting the richness of the groves of green trees as we made our final approach on an El Al flight, the Jewish music that came over the intercom (the theme from *Exodus, Roshinkes Mit Mandeln and Heveinu Shalom Aleichem*), the applause when we touched down and the large menorah that came into view as we taxied toward the terminal at Ben Gurion Airport outside of Tel Aviv. At the same time, there was the visible presence of soldiers standing guard to make sure that we would be safe, a sight that we would see throughout our travels just as later we would see young men in uniform walking on the streets or shopping with Uzi machine guns slung over their shoulders.

Sadly, the country has had to be in a constant state of alert since its beginnings, and these were soldiers either on their way to or coming home from their military service. To this day, every young person, man or woman, must serve in Israel's Armed Forces and is subject to being called for reserve duty well into their forties, even their fifties. The only exception has been the young (and not so young) Yeshiva students who, due to a long standing policy that goes back to the beginning of the state, are permitted to place their studies before service to the nation which compassionately and ironicaly has made it possible for them to live their lives and protects them. Attempts are finally being made to rectify what can only be described as a shameful state of affairs as these words are being written.

I often think about a particularly joyless Purim in 1974 when, during my visit with a group of congregants, a white booklet was issued with the names of all who had fallen during the Yom Kippur War. There were 2656 deaths out of a population of less than three million. If a similar percentage of Americans had fallen in battle, measured against our population, their number would have approximated 200,000, far more than died in combat during Vietnam. There was literally no one in the entire land who had not lost a relative, a neighbor or a friend. Such is the Israeli way of life and alas, all too often, death. Still, it is the Israeli way, perhaps because it is the Jewish way, never to let despair conquer resolve and hope. It is part of what makes Israel such an amazing land and Israelis such an extraordinary people.

While we travelled the length and breadth of the land during that first trip, the unquestionable highlight was our visit to the famous *Kotel*, the last-standing section of the Wall which surrounded King Solomon's Temple. It was on a Friday night. We had welcomed Shabbat with prayer and with a sumptuous meal at the historic King David Hotel. Afterwards, several of us made our way to the Jaffa Gate after which we followed the cobblestone path through the, by now, closed Arab market turning here and there until we came upon the brightly lit plaza at the end of which stood the enormous Western Wall. There were only a few black coated Jews standing and rocking in prayer guarded by a lone Israeli soldier, ready to risk his life for them if need be even though he in no way shared their religious values. When I first saw the Wall, I was overcome with emotion. The tears began to flow from my eyes (they still do each time I come upon it). I do not understand why for I was not raised to revere it or even imbued with a deep love for Israel. But the Wall has power that can only be described as coming from a mystical source and I experienced an overwhelming spiritual moment. Never had my Jewish connection been as strong. It was as if four thousand years of Jewish history with all of its suffering and pain had welled up and overflowed and it is true, as Shakespeare has written: There are *sermons in stones.* These stones talk to us. They talk of a people, their suffering, and their will to live and to overcome all of the forces that sought to destroy them. Above all they talk of the longing for that time when Jerusalem will be, as its name implies, a city of peace for all of its inhabitants, a place where the prayers of all who touch them or leave notes in their crevices will be fulfilled.

Brenda and I came home transformed. Not only had we encountered the world of our ancient past which came alive in an almost indescribable way but we felt a thriving, living present. Here was a people reborn out of the ashes who knew of the despair of yesterday but replaced it with faith in today and hope in tomorrow. To be sure, the Israel of the twenty-first century has lost some of its youthful idealism even as our United States no longer is marked by the same pioneering spirit that drove the founding fathers. But she remains as her national anthem proclaims, the hope, *HaTikvah.* And we and our children have the responsibility to see that she remains so, for she is truly our *hope* as well as our strength.

DISCOVERING FAMILY

I t was on that first trip to Israel that I had another encounter that was to have a major impact on my life. I met Kissinger relatives, of whose existence I had very little knowledge, and began to discover my family roots. It is an encounter that began while I was stationed at Clark Air Base and was contacted by a second cousin of my father's who lived in Israel, Martin Kissinger. Now I would meet him in person for the first time as well as another older cousin, Max. That meeting was to lead to a wonderful friendship and the discovery of my family tree which Martin had begun trace and to set down.

Members of the Kissinger family who were wise enough to escape from Hitler's clutches while there was still time had fled to all the corners of the earth. Some went to South America, some to Portugal, some, like my father, to the USA. Still others like one of my father's brothers Kurt, and like Martin and his cousins Ernst and Max, went to Israel during the days of the British Mandate when immigration was restricted but possible. It was from there, after World War II that Martin travelled back and forth to Europe and other parts of the world dealing in dry goods. He was, by his own description, in the *schmatte* business. It was on his trips to Germany, that he began to visit the town halls where very efficient German bureaucrats had established records of births and deaths going back to the 18th century and perhaps even earlier. In the 18th century, when Jews began to acquire surnames, a certain Meyer ben Loeb (b. 1767), living in a Spa known as Bad Kissingen, about an hour's drive from Nuremberg where I was born, took on the name Kissinger and gave our family its name.

By the time Brenda and I met Martin and his lovely wife Ruth, he had, as it turns out, with the help of my father among others, but unbeknownst to me, hand-written a fairly accurate and up-to-date family tree that extended from the time of Meyer ben Loeb, and traced all of the descendants of Meyer, their wives and children down to my children's generation. There were already hundreds of names on his tree giving me access to a family I had not known existed. It was an eye opening and exciting experience for me. Meyer had married at least twice fathering twelve children from both wives. Thus there are two branches of the Kissinger family who share a common progenitor but come from different mothers. Among others, I could see for the first time how I was related to the famous Henry Kissinger who came from the line of Meyer's second wife while my father (and Martin) were descended from the first wife. My father and Henry shared a great, great grandfather and thus were fourth cousins making me Henry's fourth cousin once removed. As I pointed out in an article I wrote for the American Jewish Archives titled *How Henry Kissinger Became My Cousin,* this did not impress Henry very much (he has shown little interest in family) but it always makes for good conversation.

As Martin got on in years, a wonderful thing happened. A younger cousin (my children's generation) by the name of Elizabeth Levy (whose grandmother, Bella Wallach z"l, was a Kissinger- an older first cousin to Henry), took it upon herself to continue the work Martin had begun. Elizabeth, who had grown up in Boston, and made *aliyah*, not only expanded on Martin's work in breadth and depth but put our entire *Stammbaum* (Family Tree) on computer. With her genealogical savvy and detective skills, she found members of our family not known to Martin in Israel and throughout the world, recorded their names with those of spouses, children and grandchildren, until today. There are well over a thousand names contained therein. In addition to the schematic, she created a narrative with biographical data and pictures and, best of all, an index by name and country so that one can find relatives in far off places wherever one journeys.

The discovery of family beyond the immediate boundaries of parents, uncles and aunts has been an enormously enriching (one might even say spiritual) experience and has not only connected me to people I might otherwise never have met, but it has helped me to know more about who I am. Most extraordinary was the discovery, alluded to earlier, that many of my ancestors were Jewish teachers so that the profession I had chosen, seemingly from out of the blue, may have been imbedded in my genetic profile all along. Equally rewarding is the fact that at least one of my sons, Evan, his wife and children, have also found great meaning in their extended family. During one of our trips to Israel while Evan was still a child, he spent several days with Martin and Ruth while Brenda and I travelled around the country with our group. And to this day, he maintains relationships with far-off cousins in a way that the family might stay intact. His daughters, I am happy to say, are similarly inclined.

As these words are written, there have been three Kissinger reunions. The first and most dramatic not only because it was the first but because it was held in our place of origin, Bad Kissingen, Germany, brought sixty of us together in 2005 for an amazing time of discovery and nostalgia. For four days we shared history, learned how we were related and visited places where our forebears had lived before the horrific days which drove us out of our natural homestead. For me a highlight came during a side trip to Nuremberg when we were invited, by its present inhabitants, to enter an apartment that had been inhabited by my father's father during his youth a century ago. The couple residing there had actually peeled off layers of paint and plaster to uncover a beautiful ceiling decorated with architectural elements dating back to those halcyon days. What a thrill to have walked up the stairs trod by the grandfather who died when I was not quite two and to stand where he must have stood.

Three years later, in 2008, over one hundred of us, spanning the entire secular to religious spectrum, gathered in Israel for our second reunion. Many had not come to the first reunion in Germany as a matter of principle, having vowed not to return to the land from which they were driven in which so many Jews were murdered. Given the liberal Jewish practices of all of the Kissingers known to me, it was a great surprise to learn that many of our family members in Israel are quite Orthodox. They, of course, are the ones with the most children. During that reunion, we collected enough money to be able to dedicate a grove of trees to the memory of the man who facilitated our coming together, even after death, Martin Kissinger. He undoubtedly would have *kvelled* had he known what the research which he initiated made possible.

The third, in 2012 saw forty of us gather in New York City for a day before going to the Catskills where we joined with other, non-Kissinger, German Jews who originated in the sister cities Nuremberg and Furth (not far from where the Kissingers originated) and were holding their tenth reunion. What a powerful statement! We former refugees and their descendants, now already three and four generations removed from the ravages of the Holocaust, have not permitted Hitler to obliterate memories of the richness of the culture from which we were exiled. We still look to it with warmth, for it helped to fashion who we are. Brenda and I have attended four of those extraordinary Nuremberg- Furth gatherings which always end with a memorial service that I conduct. The theme of the most recent gathering explains why, after so many years, we still come together: *We live in the present. We learn from the past. We dream of the future.*

Those N-F reunions are due to the efforts of an extranordinary man, now in his nineties, Frank Harris by name. My God grant him long life.

THE RETIREMENT YEARS

As the old saying goes, *there is life after retirement.* I did not fully understand that as I approached my sixty-fourth birthday and announced that I would come to the end of my active rabbinate at Temple Sinai in a year's time. The confluence of a number of circumstances made the decision seem wise, however, even if it came several years earlier than I had planned. The last years had been marred by a president who made life unpleasant for me and wanted me to move on. But truth be told, the reality was also that I no longer had the energy or enthusiasm I had in my earlier years, especially when it came to relating to the younger generation of parents and their children. They were truly, as the Book of EXODUS so poignantly states referring to the biblical hero a short few years after his death, a generation that *knew not Joseph.*

Only in this case, while I was still very much alive, Joseph was me. By 1997, many of the members had not grown up with me, shared the growth pangs of the congregation, understood my vision or the unique style we had developed that made Temple Sinai a special place. I did not relate to their music or the cultural and social world in which they moved. To them, I was just the old guy who stood on the *bemah* each *Shabbat* and *Yom Tov* whom they knew only as *the rabbi,* not as a person.

Truth be told, there is a certain rhythm to congregational life which sees the involvement of one generation running its course and giving way to the next. While the context was different, ECCLESIASTES had it right when he posited that *one generation comes as another goes.* So the rabbi, once young and supported by leaders who are his contemporaries finds him/herself surrounded by a new generation with whom he or (today) she may have much less in common and who have no shared memory of those earlier times.

But more than that, I had really accomplished most of what I had set out to do. I had created a vibrant congregation over which I presided for thirty-one years, from which came dedicated Jewish men and women who had achieved prominence not only within the Reform movement nationally but who had achieved leadership roles within the broader Jewish community as well. We could boast of a beautiful worship service that was both traditional yet modern blending past and present. From 150 families without a building who greeted me when I came, we had grown to well over 700 families who inhabited a beautiful, tree filled campus of seven acres in North Miami Dade, on the shores of the Oleta River. Those acres accommodated an award-winning sanctuary and three major school buildings which housed not only our Synagogue school but also our Liberal Jewish day school, attended by children from early childhood through the eighth grade. Not many other Reform congregations had attained such a goal. Perhaps it was time to let go.

What clinched matters, however, was the offer of a Sabbatical year with full pay as a parting gift and inducement. It would be all play and no work, an offer too good to refuse. So during Rosh Hashanah in 1997, I announced that I would retire on June 30, 1998. This would be my final High Holidays as senior rabbi. Thereafter, I would become rabbi emeritus with all of the lack of responsibility that accompanies that honorary title.

My words were greeted with a degree of sadness by our friends, many of whom had been members of the temple since my early years. While they realized the announcement was imminent, it still came as something of a shock. After all, it presaged the end of an era. Now there would be someone else who would be their rabbi. Protocol dictated that the emeritus cede his authority to the incoming senior rabbi and that congregants involve the emeritus in their religious lives only with the knowledge and consent of the new rabbi so long as they remain as members of the congregation. This is not always easy to accomplish.

I had, after all, named their children, buried their parents, officiated at family *Bar* and *Bat Mitzvahs* and weddings and, in general, been present with them during significant moments in their lives not only as their religious leader but as their friend. For that relationship to suddenly end is traumatic for both and goes against the natural order of things. Emeriti sometimes feel compelled to permanently leave the community in order to ease the transition but when they don't, as was the case with me, the relationship between them and their successor frequently becomes a carefully choreographed dance. It is a wise emeritus, therefore, who seeks to help the successor to gain the confidence and respect of his or her congregants and who avoids undermining his or her authority. But it is also a wise successor who makes every effort to give the emeritus proper recognition and who encourages him to remain connected to the people to whom he was close for so much of his rabbinate without feeling threatened.

To fulfill my end of the bargain, and to make the transition easier for the new rabbi, Brenda and I left Miami as soon as my official duties ended and made our way, as always we did, to the Berkshires for the summer. Only this time, we did not come home for the High Holidays. We spent *Rosh Hashanah* in Brooklyn with Evan, Dara and our New York grandchildren at their synagogue, Union Temple. On *Yom Kippur*, we were in Westport, CT with friends who had once been members of Temple Sinai, and for *Sukkot* we returned to our Lenox house and enjoyed the fall foliage. It was the first time in thirty seven years that I did not officiate during the Days of Awe. But actually, it was liberating not having to worry about writing sermons nor having to experience all of the pressures which the season brings. And it was especially meaningful to be able to pray sitting next to my wife, children and, best of all, grandchildren; something I had missed out on for all of those years when I was in the pulpit.

We made it a point to stay away from North Miami Beach and Temple Sinai during that first year in order to give my first successor as much space as possible and to avoid hearing any complaints or comparisons to *the way we did it before*. That not only enabled Brenda and me to visit other Reform congregations on Friday nights but gave me the opportunity, as well, to experience Conservative and Orthodox worship on Saturday mornings. I became an equal opportunity davener and thoroughly enjoyed the experience of going to a different synagogue each week, especially on those Sabbaths when my son Jonathan accompanied me and sat at my side. He had become a father by then, so I had the opportunity to often see my newest granddaughter, Julia.

Having been raised in a home that was nominally Reform at best, I had very little experience in traditional synagogues during my growing up years and by the time I was ordained, I was thoroughly imbued with the only style of worship I knew, that which took place in Reform synagogues. While I understood and in fact had regularly taught the structure of the Jewish worship service with its six divisions- *Preliminary prayers, the Shema and its blessings, the Tefilah (also called, Ameedah or Shemoneh Essre), Torah, Aleynu and Kaddish* - I now began to appreciate the ordered nature of Jewish prayer as I experienced it in non-Reform settings. I came to a better understanding of where, how and why the Reform liturgists had made changes in shortening the service for reasons of aesthetic appeal as well as intellectual consistency.

But for me, prayer was poetry. I could relate to and appreciate the Jewish prayer book even when the words, taken literally, did not reflect my own belief system. Prayer was, after all, not an intellectual exercise; it was a coming together of community in celebration of Jewish life. It was as much of a horizontal experience, that is person to person, as vertical, person to God. There is much truth in the old quip: *Cohen comes to Schul to talk to God. I come to talk to Cohen.*

I enjoyed the singing and the fact that everyone felt involved. It wasn't the rabbi praying for the people, who participated only when told to read together or to answer responsively as was the style in older more staid Reform congregations. They didn't just listen silently, as one does in a concert, when the cantor sang. People sang with the *Chazan* or whoever was leading prayers (which usually wasn't the rabbi) and knew when to stand and when to sit without being told. I came to appreciate the lack of regimentation- the fact that if someone came late (only the most faithful appear at the appointed hour when the service begins) they could catch up on their own. That meant that some people might be standing while others were seated. But nobody seemed to mind.

Interestingly, during my years at Temple Sinai, I had tried to create just that kind of feeling albeit still in the context of Reform Judaism- Liberal yet with a warm, traditional feeling. I must have succeeded for strangers who came to be with us for *Bar* and *Bat Mitzvah* celebrations would sometimes assume we were a Conservative congregation and that would please me for it meant that we were perceived as being appropriately Jewish. To be sure, there was much to be said for the dignity and decorum which was the mark of the Reform service, with its tone of rationality. At its best, it evoked a sense of majesty. But if one was not careful, it could also turn into a very sterile and even church-like environment, one of the strong criticisms heaped on those congregations who self identified as Classical Reform. I would like to believe that we at Temple Sinai were ahead of the curve in moving away from such a designation.

That first year during which I was still on the payroll, although without obligations, went by very quickly. On *Shabbat* morning, I went wherever I pleased and could fit in as just another Jew at prayer although often, the rabbi or congregants would recognize me (I had after all been in the community for a long time) and make me feel very much at home, frequently honoring me with an *aliyah*. During the rest of the week, I could read, attend various meetings or spend time with Brenda and see to our personal needs and desires. All told, we had come back from the Berkshires that first summer to a delightfully pressure-free existence and the discovery that there were distinct advantages to a life of retirement which included being able to travel without having to worry about having to come back for a funeral or a *Bar Mitzvah*.

NEW OPPORTUNITIES

B ut that did not last too long. Late in 1999, I was contacted by the leaders of a small retirement congregation (they have since grown into a large active congregation) in Boynton Beach whose Rabbi was ill asking whether I might conduct services for them. At first I resisted, since I was just beginning to enjoy my new-found freedom. But they prevailed on me so from January 2000 through May, Brenda and I would travel an hour to Boynton, have Shabbat dinner in a restaurant and proceed to the temple which was in a store front to conduct services. They were sweet people, a bit older than we, for whom Friday nights at the temple were an important part of their lives. Despite the travel component which was a bit of a drag, they helped make our Sabbath Eve worship experiences very pleasant. It was nice to be needed and appreciated and from what I was told, my preaching skills had not suffered as a result of a year's hiatus. Saturday mornings, with a few exceptions, remained my own.

By that time, we had moved from our zero-lot-line house in the Island Way section of the Waterways, where we had moved in 1992, to a brand new apartment in a high rise building on the ocean, at the very end of Hollywood Beach. It was our fourth move in thirty two years: seventeen years in our first house in Highland Lakes, eight years in a newly constructed house in the California Club area, and seven in the Waterways; always in close proximity to my synagogue. Now, we went a bit further north into Broward County. It seems that each time we were ready for a paint job or some interior updating, it was easier to move rather than to endure the inconvenience. Of course, Brenda being a realtor (after working as a medical assistant and then a travel agent) gave impetus to our moves for she kept finding opportunities for us to better ourselves. But this was our first experience with high rise living.

It did not take long for us to accustom ourselves to giving up a bit of our personal freedom as required by the communal nature of condominium life. Having to wait for the elevator was a small price to pay in return for the comforts and conveniences of having someone else worry about lawns and upkeep, having immediate access to a gym and a pool and having merely to turn the front door key when we left for an extended period of time without having to worry about our property.

Our five years at Renaissance on the Ocean just south of Dania Beach Blvd. were very pleasant. We met friendly people and while we had to get used to a new area, it was only twenty minutes back to the old neighborhood. Though we did not love Hollywood (we were really Dade County people) we might have stayed longer but for two factors: the building, new though it was, was not well managed. At the same time, the monthly maintenance fee, quite affordable when we moved in, rose to a point where it was becoming uncomfortable. Again, Brenda came through and found a terrific twenty fifth floor apartment in another new building in our old Waterways neighborhood. It came with an extra one room space on the third floor called a Hobby Room which the synagogue furnished for me as a home office in lieu of promised space at the temple which was not available. I was in heaven. I could now get all of my books and files out of storage and settle into a wonderful routine which included having a private area where I could study and write (I had taught myself to type when I no longer had daily access to a secretary) and even meet with people in a counseling situation as when I interviewed young couples whom I was to marry.

The stay in Hollywood did, however result in a meaningful spiritual experience which led to my writing an article for the CCAR Journal called *In Search of a Place to Pray*. Unlike North Dade, there was not an overabundance of synagogues. The nearest *Shul* was in a small house off the Broadwalk on Hollywood Beach, a five to ten minute drive from our condo. It was totally Orthodox and peopled by a group of men most of whom were older than me, many of them Holocaust survivors. There were no *bells and whistles*; not even a rabbi or cantor except for an occasional visit by a retired rabbi spending the winter in the neighborhood. There were perhaps twenty Jews, in season a few more, who gathered to be with each other and to offer prayers to the Holy One in celebration of the Sabbath and in gratitude for having lived when so many of their family members had been murdered.

The Orthodox service was, of course strange to me for reasons mentioned earlier. We used the Art Scroll Siddur, the style and the theology of which is far from my own belief system. The God it asked me to pray to was not the One I had come to believe in. But it didn't matter. I could feel a sense of holiness. As I wrote in my article, *The people who gather to pray in that little do-it-yourself minyan are there for only three reasons: they want to be; it is Shabbat (or Yom Tov) and that is where a Jew ought to be; and they understand that regular worship is a Mitzvah that a Jew ought to fulfill.* This was not a Bar Mitzvah crowd that waited for the service to end so that they could party. It was not recalcitrant children whose equally recalcitrant parents had dropped them at the door. It was Jews who gathered to pray because the act of praying in the midst of their fellow Jews was in and of itself a fulfilling experience. Shabbat was a holy day to be spent away from the hustle and bustle of the every day. Theirs, in brief, was a world that was very different from the one I had lived in. But it was one I could appreciate even as I remained a committed Liberal Jew, both in belief and in my personal practice. Once again I came to experience what I had understood for some time; that one could be seemingly Orthodox in one's practice yet still be a Reform Jew. The determining factor was not what one did but why one did it. In this case, other considerations notwithstanding, I found what I did to be Jewishly meaningful: an affirmation not only of a Jewish God but more significantly, of Jewish peoplehood. It was the very essence of what I had come to believe as a Jew.

As a result, when we moved back to our old stamping ground in Aventura, I felt sad that I would have to give up my new found *Shul*. It didn't make sense to drive back the twenty minutes it would take, especially when there were so many congregations to choose from in the old neighborhood to which we returned. But memories of my Sabbaths there remained, even as I attended a variety of synagogues ranging from an Orthodox Young Israel congregation that was within walking distance- a ten minute walk from our Condo - to the two major Conservative congregations that were a short drive away; and of course, my own Temple Sinai which by now had its second successor rabbi. I found myself doing what I decried during my days in the active rabbinate, going from synagogue to synagogue without committing to any. But given my years of service to the Jewish community, I gave myself a pass and continue to enjoy my Sabbath mornings.

The style of worship in each, even from one Conservative to the other, is different, depending on the culture of the congregation, the predilection of the individual rabbi and the nature of the music. Congregations with older memberships tend to favor a style of worship reminiscent of what its members experienced when they were younger and reflects the area from which they came - the North East and Canada, which were more traditional. Congregations with younger memberships tend to be more open to new experiences and change. That is part of what makes being Jewish and shul hopping so much fun. But regardless of differences, what has made Jewish worship unique over the years is that wherever you go, no matter the style or the prayer book, the essential structure of the service is the same; the same section of the Torah will be read; *Kaddish*, the mourner's prayer, will be recited at the end of the service. There is great comfort in that.

In an effort to be relevant and creative, some of my Reform colleagues argue that maintaining such congruity need not be of primary concern when we are attempting to modernize the prayer book or even when selecting the Torah or *Haftarah* portion. For me, being as much in sync with what goes on in other synagogues throughout the world is an absolute principle. It strengthens us as a people and, together with our ritual calendar is our greatest unifying feature. I have long believed that one can create a meaningful worship experience without doing radical surgery on the prayer book.

What made the *Gates of Prayer* (the first major revision of the old *Union Prayer Book* in 1975) and (not long after, in 1978) its companion High

Holiday prayer book, *The Gates of Repentence*, as well as *Mishkan T'filah* (the most recent Sabbath and weekday prayer book), so significant was that they returned to the Reform liturgy some of the traditional prayers which earlier Reformers, in their zeal to shorten the service, to make it philosophically pure and appropriately modern, had omitted. A traditional Jew who worships in a Reform congregation should not feel that s/he is in a foreign place. And conversely, a Reform Jew who attends a traditional synagogue should, with proper education, be able to find his or her way in the service and not be uncomfortable. The style of worship may be different but the essential structure must be the same. No Jew should ever feel as a stranger no matter the nature of the synagogue. Happily, the days when the Reform worship service would be described as *Jewnitarian* (a play on Unitarian) because it had become so imitative of Protestant worship are gone. Today's congregants tend to be more Hebraicly literate, less doctrinaire and more open to traditional patterns of Jewish prayer. They can move rather comfortably from one stream of Judaism to another without being committed to this or that ideology. For the ideological purist, this may pose a problem. I personally, find it refreshing and believe it bodes well for the future of our people.

There have, incidentally, been several other opportunities during the years following my retirement for me to pursue my rabbinic skills in addition to the brief tenure in Boynton Beach. I spent one High Holiday period with a small Reform congregation in Central Florida which seemed to revel in the fact that they got along all year without a rabbi. I also conducted High Holiday Services for a small gay synagogue in Ft. Lauderdale while they were between rabbis. That year, *Yom Kippur* prayers ended soon after the morning service because a hurricane was bearing down on South Florida and worshippers needed to retreat to the safety of their homes. Some years later, I was asked to serve as interim rabbi for a congregation in Fort Meyers for the better part of a year beginning with *Rosh Hashanah*. While Brenda and I did not love travelling to and fro across the state by car each weekend, we thoroughly enjoyed the overall experience, especially meeting new people who appreciated our presence. The congregation had been through a difficult time with a former rabbi, and I was able to effectuate some healing.

It subsequently engaged a new rabbi and is thriving. Most recently, I have been returning to Temple Sinai sometimes to teach the Sabbath morning Torah class and sometimes to conduct services on Sabbath Eve or Sabbath morning when my successor is otherwise occupied.

But perhaps the most spiritually satisfying times have come during my annual *Yiskor* sermon on *Yom Kippur* afternoon which has been something of a tradition in recent years. Not only has that occasion provided an opportunity for me to reconnect with many of the people who were my congregants and friends in years gone by but there is something very special about that time of day as *Yom Kippur* moves into its final hours. The slowly setting sun from without, the emerging hunger pangs from within, and the strong emotions that come from remembering dear ones all unite at that time of day and contribute to a powerful religious moment. It means much to me to be part of it. So, yes, there is life after retirement and the opportunities for spiritual fulfillment continue.

THE FUTURE

So what of the future? In my lifetime, I have seen an amazing ferment in Jewish life and thought throughout the Jewish world. All three major streams of Jewish life have struggled to redefine themselves in the light of the Holocaust and the birth of Israel as well as trying to come to terms with the emergence of the women's movement. Beginning in the 1970s, there has been a veritable outpouring of liturgical creativity with the publication of new prayer books for use not only in Reform congregations but in Orthodox and Conservative synagogues as well. Reform, as usual, has taken a leadership role, especially in making prayer vocabulary gender sensitive beginning with the addition of the Mothers of Israel (Sarah, Rebecca, Leah and Rachel) to the Fathers (Abraham, Isaac and Jacob) at the beginning of the *Ameedah*, but also in the use of gender neutral language when referring to God, avoiding the use of HE whenever possible.

All but the most intransigently Orthodox have tried to address the changing role of women in what had been a patriarchal culture. They are struggling to find a place for gays and lesbians who are more freely *coming out* even as they look for ways to accommodate the increasing demand for gay marriage which has been legalized nationally. Add to the list the impact of intermarriage on the makeup of the congregation when it comes to matters of membership or the assignment of *Bema* honors to non Jewish spouses, for example, during a *Bar* or *Bat Mitzvah* service. While I occasionally had to deal with all of the above, those issues are far more commonplace today than they were during my rabbinate, when they were first beginning to come to the fore.

It should not therefore be surprising that I think about what Jewish life will be like for my grandchildren. I wonder, for example, whether the streams of Judaism representing differing approaches to Jewish thought and practice will still exist as we currently know them. Or will the lines of demarcation and individuation become more and more blurred following a trend that I find very apparent? We seem to be realigning ourselves into four divisions of which two are centrist movements and two are more extreme falling at either end of the ideological spectrum. On the center left are those who come from main line Reform, Reconstructionist and liberal Conservative congregations. On the center right are the more tradition bound Conservative congregations as well as the modern Orthodox. The former affirm a Judaism that is subject to change and development in accordance with the times even as they remain committed to and grounded in the tradition. The latter, while acknowledging the legitimacy of the former, the impact of modernism and the need for adaptability, still adhere more rigidly to the strictures of Jewish law and are less willing to change.

On the extreme left are those most radical in their reforms among them Jewish humanists and secularists for whom Jewish particularity takes second place to universal values. While maintaining a nominal Jewish connection, they do not feel as strong a tie to traditional Jewish practice or feel bound by norms set forth by the established Jewish community. Often they also lack a strong connection to Israel as the homeland of the Jewish people. My fear is that their children will find little reason to remain connected to their historic roots or to care about Jewish survival especially if they are the product of intermarriage.

And on the extreme right are the ultra Orthodox- the *Hasidim* and the *Haredim*- who declare theirs to be the only legitimate and authentic expression of Judaism and who, as a result, seek to delegitimize all other streams of Jewish life. While I am fearful that the ultra liberalism of those on the extreme left may easily lead to assimilation, intermarriage and a weakening of and even disappearance of Judaism over the generations, I am equally concerned that the triumphalism and narrowness of the extreme right, with its fundamentalist theology, is little less than a return to a Middle Ages mentality. It is no different from that which one finds in sections of the Islamic world.

As I read about attempts by the so-called, ultra religious to (literally) consign women to the back of the bus in Israel, and the arrest of women for wearing a prayer shawl and singing the words of the *Shma* at the Western Wall, even though in the section designated for women, I wonder whether this is the same religion that I have practiced all of my life and worry that it will cause otherwise committed Jews to throw up their hands in disgust and to want no more to do with our people. There is no reasoning with ultra rightists who are convinced that only they know the true path to the Divine and who think nothing of throwing stones, even at children, when they feel their rules are being violated. There is a mean-spirited anger and hostility which seethes in the hearts of the men who adhere to such an ideology. While they remain a part of our Jewish tapestry, we must not allow them to gain power for their force is destructive.

Instead, I am hopeful that those of us in the center left and center right will find ways to cooperate with each other in pursuit of a strong and vibrant Jewish way of life even as we function within the real world of the twenty first century with all of its challenges. While one continues to hope that those at either extreme will find their way back to the center, it may become necessary, at some point, for those in the center, whether among the liberals or traditionalists, to declare that we, even with our differences, represent *normative Judaism,* and that those at the extremes have removed themselves from the mainstream. At the very least, we must do all we can to marginalize them so that they wield no influence outside of their narrow, self imposed, boundaries.

It will also be necessary for our fellow Jews in Israel to awaken to the realization that their *Haredi* population is not only endangering Jewish religious life but even the democratic character of our beloved Jewish state. Just as extreme elements in the Arab world, among other of their goals, are pushing for a return to *Sharia* Law and thus the complete disenfranchisement of women, together with political rule by their religious leaders, so too would the *Haredim* like to see a return to rule by *Halacha*, albeit not as it has evolved in a liberal way but in its narrowest iteration. Unhappily, too few Israelis seem yet to have awakened to that reality and are still closing their eyes as personal rights and especially a woman's right to openly and proudly practice Judaism as an equal, are denied. There are elements within the *non-Haredi* religious community who know better and are well intentioned even as there are such elements within the more secular population. But until they join forces in protest, things will get worse before they improve, and the Israel that my generation grew up with and loved will become a distant memory.

In a most insightful article published in the New York Times, Avraham Burg, former speaker of the Knesset and once head of the Jewish Agency, famous son of an even more famous father, Yosef Burg, who gained renown as head of the National Religious Party during the 1970's and 80's, contrasts two worlds. The one is that in which he grew up, in which *Americans and Israelis talked about democracy, human rights, respect for other nations and human solidarity…an age of dreamers and builders who sought to create a new world without prejudice, racism or discrimination.* The other is an Israel and America today, *joined together not by a covenant of humanistic values but rather a new set of mutual interests: war, bombs, fear, threats and trauma.*

It is a vision of that former world that drew me to Judaism and which, through my rabbinate and my life I have sought to create and which I still believe is attainable. It is that kind of world that I would like my grandchildren to discover as they grow into adulthood. So permit me to address the final section of my journey to them: to Ava Margot (Aviva Margolit), Elizabeth Berenice (Elisheva Bracha), Julia Sarah (Itta Sarah), and Max David (Moshe David) for my hope is that my journey will be continued by them.

TO MY GRANDCHILDREN WHO CONTINUE THE JOURNEY

Y ou probably don't give it too much thought, but you too have begun your spiritual journey. In a way, I suppose those journeys began when I officiated at the marriages of your parents, a privilege that few grandfathers get to experience. While the venues for each ceremony were far apart and very different in style - one wedding took place in a small synagogue in White Plains, New York and the other in a country club in Boca Raton, Florida - they had much in common. Each featured beautiful brides, Evan's Dara, and Jonathan's Wendy, who were chosen by your handsome fathers because of their intelligence and warmth, and because they came from loving Jewish homes. Each was marked by a spirit of joy and fulfillment that derived from the knowledge that the lives of all of the parents, the Kingsleys, the Meyers and the Brenners, were being enriched by the coming-together of their children and the accompanying extended families that resulted from each relationship. Most of all, both were times of extraordinary emotion for me, standing in my role as the father of the groom next to your beaming grandmother and, also, as the officiating rabbi. Of the hundreds of weddings I solemnized during my rabbinical lifetime, these were the most special. If I felt an enormous sense of historical continuity at the circumcisions of your fathers, as described earlier, here I felt an even greater sense of gratification as new families were born and hopes for a Jewish future enhanced.

Your parents did not disappoint. They have reared you into a life of *Torah and good deeds*, as set forth in the prayers recited when you were given your Hebrew names. They have, as Judaism demands, imbued you with the importance of learning both Jewish and secular. The fact that learning is considered a religious value in Jewish life was demonstrated when you became *Bar* and *Bat Mitzvah* around the time of your thirteenth birthdays and displayed your budding wisdom by delivering a thoughtful *D'var Torah*. It was also evidenced by the excellent grades you have earned over the years in your various schools which have helped you gain acceptance into outstanding institutions of higher learning.

But *wisdom without works is like a tree without roots*, taught an ancient sage, which is to say that learning alone does not make one a rounded human being. Your parents and teachers have thus encouraged you to be sensitive to humanistic values – the need to put your learning to use for the betterment of humankind. That is what is meant by *maasim tovim,* the good deeds that must go along with *Torah*. The purpose of the *mitzvah* project that was part of your *Bar* and *Bat Mitzvah* requirement and the community service you had to perform as part of your secular education both are directed to that end. I firmly believe that what makes us most Jewish is, at the same time, what makes us most human and pray that you allow our humanistic values to permeate your lives.

It remains, however, for the third element of that naming prayer spoken at the beginning of your Jewish journey, also to be fulfilled: the hope for *Huppah,* a Jewish marriage under the wedding canopy, so that the journey might continue into the next generation. I think I can safely speak for all of your grandparents in saying that we pray to live long enough for that to come to pass.

All of this is by way of saying that you are heirs to an extraordinary tradition to which you were connected soon after birth when your parents gave you a name. Each name is a reminder of someone in your family's past. It was not a matter of choice for you then but by giving you a Hebrew name, your parents indicated their intention to raise you with an awareness that you are here by virtue of those who have come before and whose legacy it is yours to continue as, one day, God willing, you establish your own family. For, while we Jews are inheritors of a unique value system that has survived centuries of pain and persecution, we are also all about family and continuity. The words of our liturgy *L'dor vador nagid gawdlecha,* are meant not only to remind us to continually praise God's greatness but that we are indeed linked from *generation to generation* in a bond that can only be broken if we consciously, or even unconsciously separate ourselves from it. My fervent hope is that each in your own way will follow along the path set by your forebears as you embark on your own personal journey. With that in mind, here are some of the things I have learned over the years which I hope will give you some guidance along the way.

Perhaps the best place to start is with our calendar. We Jews are unique in that we live not only by the western calendar which is set by the rotation of the earth around the sun, but by a Jewish calendar that functions according to the phases of the moon and determines the beginning and end of each of our festival days. It is those festivals which are, for the most part, celebrations of our history but, which are also the source of our values – the signposts which tell us what should be important in our lives; what it is that makes us Jewish and therefore special. I think that is what Rabbi Samson Raphael Hirsch, a nineteenth century German rabbi who is generally associated with the beginnings of what we call Modern Orthodoxy, meant when he said that the *calendar is the catechism of the Jew.* It helps shape who we are.

Thus, Passover, our spring festival, is both the story of our struggle to be free of Egyptian Bondage and a reminder of our obligation to pursue freedom and justice for all the enslaved people of the world, whether that enslavement is political or the result of hunger, poverty or even debilitating illness which saps our spiritual as well as physical strength. The *Seder* is a wonderful opportunity for family to be together and to share not only our common history and heritage but our personal stories as well. Properly managed it should speak to different generations in different ways. I know the temptation is always to be done with telling and to get to the eating but what is the rush? Savor the moment. It comes but once each year and is very special. And for goodness sakes, don't forget that the first and seventh days are meant as full days of celebration. That means no work or school and attendance at synagogue.

For me that is as much a part of the holiday as not eating bread or bread products for seven days.

Only seven weeks later *Shavuot* comes to teach us of the importance of law (one of the translations of Torah; the other is *Teaching*) and loyalty; that without a moral law or teaching, there can be no real freedom but only chaos and confusion. Is there a story more dramatic than the giving of Torah on Mt. Sinai amidst thunder and lightning? Are there more compelling words than those, also read on that day, spoken by the Moabite daughter-in-law (Ruth) of a Jewish mother-in-law (Naomi) when she affirmed her newly acquired faith by saying *Where you go, I will go; where you stay, I will stay. Your People will be my People. Your God will be my God?* Sadly, Shavuot is a forgotten holiday for many Jews. Yet it is in many ways the most relevant and modern. It speaks of those very values which are the foundation of a just, fair and peaceful society; not only the famous Ten Commandments, but respect for one's neighbor and for human life, concern for the poor and downtrodden in our midst, the widow and the orphan.

The fall brings us the lofty High Holidays, *Rosh Hashanah* and *Yom Kippur,* with their themes of forgiveness and the ever present possibility of new beginnings. Unlike Classical Christianity which views man as born with a sinful nature needing God's grace to provide salvation, Judaism understands that while we all err, we are given the chance, each year, to right the wrongs we may have committed and to set a new course for ourselves: that *Teshuvah, Tefilah, Tzedakah (*Repentance, Prayer and Righteousness*) avert the evil of God's decree.* What happens in our world is not pre-ordained but depends on how we relate to each other and the manner in which we live our lives.

Only five days after the conclusion of those *Ten Days of Awe,* as the very ethereal period from *Rosh Hashanah* to *Yom Kippur* is called, because it speaks of life and death and offers the hope that we may be well inscribed in the *Book of Life,* comes the dramatically different, earthbound holiday of *Sukkot.* It is marked by a dual message: *Thanksgiving,* suggested by the fall harvest, on the one hand; *Human Frailty* as dramatized by the flimsy *Sukkah*, on the other. The mood of the season is enhanced by the reading, on the Sabbath between the first and last days of the Festival, of the brilliant book of ECCLESIASTES. It's very first sentence, suggests that *all is vanity,* and later reminds us that *for everything there is a time and a purpose to every season under heaven...* Remarkably, *Sukkot* is the only holiday on which we are specifically commanded to rejoice, a forced reminder perhaps of the one supreme mandate in Jewish life: that a Jew must never despair, even in the darkest of times. *Sukkot* underlines that conviction.

Earlier in this memoir, I wrote of how my earliest Jewish memories, happy ones it should be said, are associated with *Sukkot*: among them are its smells, colors and ceremonies, the waving of *lulov* and *etrog,* the tasting of sweet wine and the act of *Sukkah*-building itself. These are superseded only as *Sukkot* ends on *Simhat Torah* when children march around the sanctuary following behind the Torah scrolls with flags and miniature Torahs held in their little hands, creating an experience that lasts for a lifetime. The idea is for us to create happy Jewish memories for our children while they are young. Those memories are the stuff of Jewish survival.

But not all memories, of course, are happy ones. Over the years we have also learned to remember times that brought us much pain albeit never to a point of wallowing in those memories. Haman the Persian vizier would have annihilated us had not Mordecai and Esther come to the rescue. Yet our response on *Purim* is to read the story in the *Megillah*, to laugh and give gifts to the poor. Haman is gone and we are still here! Later, the Syrian Greeks thought they could do away with us by keeping us from the light of Torah and forbidding us to observe our precious *Shabbat* or to follow our dietary restrictions- the laws of *Kashrut*. They failed because our faith was too strong. The Maccabees led an uprising against the mighty King Antiochus and prevailed. We remember by reading from the Torah each Sabbath and by kindling lights for eight days on *Hanukah* to celebrate the miracle of our victory.

Of course the worst of the attempts to destroy us came at the hands of the German dictator, Adolf Hitler, who almost succeeded by overseeing the murder of 6 million Jews, 1.5 million of them children. We who survive remember our victims each *Yom Hashoah* (Holocaust Day) and then rejoice eight days later on *Yom Haatzm'ut* (Independence Day) when we celebrate the birthday of Israel, born out of the ashes of the Holocaust in 1948. Those two events, the Holocaust and the creation of the state of Israel were the two most important Jewish historical events of my lifetime and perhaps for many lifetimes to come. They have helped to shape the Jewish life that you inherit.

You have grown up learning of those events from your teachers and from parents and grandparents who may have told you stories of relatives who perished during those horrible years between 1933, the year Hitler first became Chancellor of Germany, and 1945, when World War II finally ended. They are far-away stories not only because they happened long before you were born but also because, except for my paternal grandmother, Else Kissinger, of blessed memory, who was transported to a camp called, Isbica in March 1942 where she is believed to have perished at the age of sixty three, most of the members of my immediate family were fortunately spared. So too were the German parents of Oma Karin Meyers who had the wisdom to emigrate to the United States with their daughters in time to escape from the clutches of the Nazis. My paternal grandfather, Isadore died in 1935 before things got really bad. My maternal grandparents were able to emigrate at the last moment and joined us in New York City in 1940 where they lived out their lives: my grandfather Henry Maier lived only for four more years till 1944 but my grandmother Tony into her eighties, long enough to hold her great grandson Evan Moshe in her arms when we brought him home from the Philippines in 1962.

You have also been blessed in not having to experience anti-Semitism for you live in a wonderful land which has been home to us for many years; We Jews have flourished here, and are made to feel welcome. We no longer have to worry, as did my father, of anyone knowing we are Jewish so that we would be kept from a job. We need not be concerned that attendance at a certain college might be denied because there are quotas that keep Jews out – a common occurrence prior to World War II.

At the same time, I need to add a word of caution for there have been other times in our history, for example during the Golden Age of Spain and even in pre-World War II Germany, where Jews believed themselves to have become an integral part of the population proudly placing their Spanish or German citizenship above their Jewish identity only to be rudely awakened when people they thought were their friends turned on them. The sad reality, if history has taught us anything, is that we must remain forever vigilant and that ultimately we can only rely on ourselves and each other.

The reality is also that we are safest when the society we live in is free and open. That means we must stand with those who fight against attempts to lessen our freedoms or would take away our right to free expression. We must be on the side of those who work for a society in which there is equal justice for all, black as well as white, male as well as female, gay and straight, the stranger from another land, the hungry, homeless and forsaken as well the home born and well-to-do. It means we must take seriously the teachings of the biblical prophets who admonished us to care for the widow, the poor and the orphan and that we must never, as the Torah teaches us, *stand idly by while our neighbor bleeds.* The most important lesson to be learned from the Holocaust is that the greatest sin is to be silent when others suffer or are victimized. That is what we mean when we utter what has become the mantra of Jewish Life in the twenty-first century, *Never Again,* and why we are so protective of Israel in every possible way, at times to a fault.

I have left the most important holiday for last, the one that comes each week. I speak of course of the Sabbath. A great Jewish writer by the name of Asher Ginsburg, better known by his pen name, Ahad HaAm (one of the people), who lived in Russia during the latter part of the nineteenth and early part of the twentieth century once wrote: *More than Jews have kept the Sabbath, the Sabbath has kept the Jews.* By that he meant that no institution has been more central to Jewish survival than the seventh day of the week which comes at sundown on Friday evening and departs when three stars appear in the sky on Saturday night.

It was to be a reminder that even God stopped work after six days of creating and rested on the seventh day. Thus it became the first great freedom holiday for on it everyone was to rest, rich and poor, young and old, male and female, servant and master. Unlike most societies in ancient days where a person's time belonged to whoever was paying his or her wages, the Sabbath came along to teach that at least during one day each week, every person was to be in control of his/her own time. The Sabbath is, therefore, as the *Kiddush* reminds us, not only *a reminder of Creation* (*Zicharon L'maasei B'reshit*) but also of *the Exodus from Egypt* (*Zecher L'Tziat Mitzrayim*) where, as slaves, time was not our own. It is the gift of the Jewish people to a world in which every religion has, in one way or another, adopted the concept of a day of rest. In the United States, it became an important principle for the Labor Movement (many of whose early leaders were Jews) which fought against the exploitation of laborers by insisting on a finite work week because every worker had a right to time off for renewal. Without a day of rest, we are, after all, no better than slaves.

But for us, the Sabbath became more than merely a day when work came to a halt. It became an important family day. At the least, it is a time for families to sit around a specially set dinner table on Friday evening and to reaffirm ties to each other and to their faith as they light candles, sing *Kiddush* and as parents bless their children with the ancient words of the Priestly benediction. I remember so well a Protestant Naval chaplain telling me how much he envied Jews because they found a way through such institutions as the Sabbath to strengthen family ties.

More optimally, the Sabbath provides an even stronger tie to our tradition on Saturday morning in synagogue where the study of Torah is the centerpiece of the worship service. I wrote earlier of how I had a true sense of the Sabbath for the first time when I attended a youth conclave and what an extraordinary experience that was for me. But better still was it when I was able to bring it into my mother and father's home during their latter years and later into the home I myself established with your grandmother- the home in which your fathers grew up.

Much has changed dramatically during my life's journey. I refer not only to the amazing additions which technology has brought into our lives which were the stuff of science fiction not that long ago: Cell phones, computers, i Phones, i Pads and all of the electronic gadgets that have become so much a part of our daily existence. Consider that television was not part of my childhood or the fact that color TV was just beginning to make its way into homes during the early years of my marriage. Equally and perhaps even more dramatic has been the changing role of women in our society away from their traditional roles as *helpmates* to men (see the Creation story in the Bible where Eve is referred to as an *ezer k'negdo* to Adam) and at the same time, the acceptance and normalization of gay marriage. Both together have led us to an entirely new understanding of just what we mean by home and family.

Still, even given that new reality, I am as convinced as ever that while our understanding of what constitutes a family may have changed, the underlying importance of the family and its centrality in the maintenance of the life of the Jewish people is unchanged. It is the home in which both parents have shared a common faith and heritage which, in turn, they have transmitted to their children, that has been our greatest strength and our most potent survival tool. Jewish days of celebration and commemoration are not meant to be experienced alone. They are meant to be celebrated in community, a community which begins in microcosm around the dinner table in the home which the tradition considers a *small sanctuary* and extends from there to the community of like-minded believers outside of the home (the synagogue) and from one generation to the next.

While it is not the only reason, that is why the choice of a mate becomes so important for when he or she does not share that common belief and value system, it is like marrying someone who speaks a different language and makes rearing a Jewish child much more difficult, if not impossible.

Throughout the years of my rabbinate, I like all of my Orthodox and Conservative colleagues and most Reform colleagues as well, refused to officiate at marriages where both parties were not Jewish. It is not that the non-Jewish partner was somehow inferior or unworthy as a human being or that I did not believe in the reality of the love that two people may have felt for each other. But I could not in good conscience publicly sanction a relationship which would in all likelihood have led to a weakening of the fabric of Jewish life because a Jewish home needs the presence of Jewish spouses sharing the cycle of Jewish life and propitiating Jewish values. The sad fact of the matter is that with rare exceptions, children of intermarriages do not grow up with the same Jewish commitment as children of in-marriages. Even when the attempt is made to raise such children as Jews, their intermarriage rate tends to be higher than that of in-marriages and their children (the grandchildren of the original couple) are often lost to the Jewish people.

One of my favorite answers to the question of *who is a Jew* is: *someone who has Jewish grandchildren.* While it was said half jokingly, there is much truth in that quip. It stands alongside another of my favorite comments ascribed to Rabbi Emil Fackenheim who escaped from Germany for England in 1939 after having spent a month in the Dachau Concentration Camp after Kristallnacht. From England he went to Canada where he served as a pulpit Rabbi and then, after earning a PH.D, became a professor of philosophy at the University of Toronto before making *aliyah* and spending his last nineteen years in Israel. He spent much of his life devoted to the study of the Holocaust and famously taught that there was a 614th commandment incumbent on the modern Jew who treasures his or her Judaism, on top of the traditional 613 (*Taryag Mitzvot*) as set forth in the Torah: *To never give Hitler a posthumous victory!* Since it was the goal of Hitler to make the world *Judenrein* - that is to rid the world of all Jews - it became, in Fackenheim's eyes, the special, holy responsibility of all Jews to ensure the survival of the Jewish people and of Jewish life. It is a responsibility to which much of my life has been devoted. It informs my commitment to the synagogue, to the Jewish community, to Jewish values and Jewish observance as well as to the land of Israel which is the most dramatic symbol of our having prevailed over those who would rather we be no more.

FINAL THOUGHTS

One of the very special passages that is found prior to the recitation of *Kaddish* in the Gates of Repentance, our High Holiday prayer book, contains the words *and life is a Journey: from childhood to maturity and youth to age; from innocence to awareness and ignorance to knowing… from weakness to strength or strength to weakness and often back again…* part of a meditation by the late Rabbi Alvin Fine. The older I get, the more those words resonate. I realize that our lives seldom move along straight lines and indeed, as I review my spiritual journey, I am grateful for the moments of victory, success, joy and exultation, many of them richer because they were shared with dear ones. But I also remember the moments of failure, frustration and regret when I would have liked to have had a *do-over* as in those childhood days when everything seemed like a game. That is of course not possible. Moreover, there is so much that I still don't know or understand and never will; so much still to learn.

Yet part of the joy of growing older is growing out of old ideas and being able to embrace the new, the more so when it enables us to bring more compassion and wisdom into our world. Is that not the reason that the Eternal One placed us on this earth? One of my favorite Hasidic tales has the Rebbe asking his *Hasidim*, whether they loved him. After many assurances that, of course, they loved him and how could he even ask such a question, he still wasn't satisfied with their answer and responded: *Do you know what gives me pain?*

I would like to believe that we Jews who have suffered so much throughout our history understand that better than most and therefore have been responsive when any person or any group cries out for help.

It is why we, especially those who view Judaism through liberal eyes, have been at the forefront in the fight for social justice and in efforts to further the cause of peace and human dignity.

It is also why, despite our personal setbacks, we view the future with hope that tomorrow will somehow be better than today. The Messiah or Messianic Age, after all will come at the end of history, not as Christianity teaches, at the beginning. *Life is a journey*. It is open-ended. Change is not only possible. It is inevitable, built into the universe itself. The future is determined not by some hidden power but by the choices we make; by the way we live our lives from day to day and year to year. In a sense, Shalom Aleichem's fabled *Tevyah the Dairyman* was speaking not only for his own generation but for all time when he said to his beloved wife in a moment of family crisis a century ago, *It's a new world Golda.*

But as Tevyah also understood so well, there is that which cannot change and must not change. There is tradition. There is legacy. There are family values and history that deserve to be preserved and transmitted. It is some of that which I have sought to capture by setting forth the memory of my spiritual journey as it has unfolded during these eight decades. It has been far from a perfect journey. But it has filled my life with meaning and for the most part, great joy. I hope that those who chose to read it will have gained an insight not only into who I was but into the extraordinary era in which I lived.

Ralph P. Kingsley

HANUKAH 5776 (2015)

APPENDIX:
PUBLISHED ARTICLES

Ralph P. Kingsley | THE BUBER-ROSENZWEIG

TRANSLATION OF THE BIBLE

Since the new Torah translation sponsored by the Jewish Publication Society has brought to the fore the various problems facing the Biblical translator, it might be of interest to examine another Bible translation, accomplished in an earlier period, in a different language, and with a different goal in mind than that which motivated Dr. Harry Orlinsky and his committee.

In 1925, Martin Buber and Franz Rosenzweig began working on a new German Bible Translation. They worked together until the death of Rosenzweig in 1929, after which Buber continued alone.

Their translation is of interest for many reasons. Not the least of these is that both these men have had a marked influence on contemporary Jewish thought and theology, but more important is the fact that their entire approach to translation was unique. Unlike the new JPS translation which aims to make the ancient Biblical text as intelligible to the contemporary reader as possible, using the latest advances in Biblical scholarship, and by means of a modern, easily comprehensible idiomatic style, Buber and Rosenzweig hoped to be able to come close not only to the essential meaning of the Hebrew text, but to reproduce its classical style as well. In effect, they wanted the contemporary reader to perceive the Bible in German, in the same manner in which Jews, throughout the centuries, have perceived it in Hebrew.

In a collection of essays called *Die Schrift und Ihre Verdeutschung* Buber and Rosenzweig set forth their "method." Perhaps their most important premise — that upon which their entire philosophy of translation is built — is that the Bible is a recording of the spoken word. Long before the Bible became the כתוב it was the קְרִיאָה. "Alles in der Schrift ist echte Gesprochenheit," says Rosenzweig.

Buber and Rosenzweig speak of "Paronomasie" (paronomasia or word play), in general, and the use of the "Leitwort" (key-word) in particular. Under the general heading of Paronomasia, come such effects as root repetition וַיֵּצֵא יָצֹא, or the use of alliteration to achieve a special effect, or to enforce a meaning. For example, in the phrase פָּצְתָה אֶת פִּיהָ the double use of the plosive פ supports vocally the violence of the earth's "opening her mouth" to swallow the blood of Abel.

The key-word is a particular manifestation of the more general paronomasia. "Leitwort" is a word used in several different contexts, or within a specific passage, to enforce a certain idea or to help the reader draw certain conclusions. The expression לֶךְ לְךָ is used twice in the Abraham story — once when God commands him to leave home, and once when God commands him to go to an unknown place. Both times the answer is וילך. The use of the root and the repetition of specific forms of this root presumably help the reader to make a connection between these episodes, and to see Abraham as a man of considerable faith who trustingly heeds the command of God. Similarly, Buber thinks it no accident that both Noah and Abraham are תמים and that both התהלך with God (a fact which the Midrash also points out).

These two translators were conscious of an inner rhythm of words, phrases and ideas which was unique to Biblical style. More important, they felt that this style was interwoven with what the text tried to say. For Buber and Rosenzweig, therefore, it became very important not only to translate words properly, but also to recapture as correctly as possible the style and rhythm of the text.

This they tried to do in a number of ways. First, they sought to recreate assonances and alliterations. On a simple level שוב אשוב and ידע תדע are given as "Kehren Kehren," and "Merken sollst du merken." On a more difficult level, the phrase וירח יהוה את ריח ניחח is translated: "Da roch ER den Ruch der Befriedung." Here, Buber tried to do several things. He wanted to get the sense of euphony, the alliterative effect of וירח and ריח and the ח sounds. He also wanted to point to a possible root connection between נוח and ניחח, feeling that the word ניחח contained both the notion of trying to pacify God, Who had just sent the flood, and of trying to put Him at rest (hence נוח) as well. He finds both desired connotations in the word Befriedung and even captures the

genitive force of ריח ניחח in German. Such examples can, of course, be multiplied.

A second characteristic was the attempt to translate a specific Hebrew word with the same German equivalent throughout, even to the point of attempting to imitate the Hebrew word construction in German. If the root of a certain key word, used in several contexts, was to "ring a bell," so to speak, in the mind of the reader (in German) it obviously had to appear in recognizable and knowable form. At the same time, it was important to differentiate between related concepts which undoubtedly had distinctive meanings originally, but which of late had been similarly translated.

צדקה and משפט, for example, have both been translated as "justice" in English. Buber and Rosenzweig attempted consistently to render them by two different root words or families of words. "Recht" is chosen to correspond to the root שפט, and "Wahr" is thought to come closest to צדק. Thus, such variants of שפט as שָׁפַט, מִשְׁפָּט, שׁוֹפְטִים etc., will be translated by such German variants as "Richter," "Recht," "Gerichtet," "Gerichtsacher," "Gerichtsanspruch" and the like, while "Wahrheit," "Wahrhaftigkeit," and "Wahrspruch" can be formed for the צדק family. Specifically, צדקה would be "die Bewährung" and צדיק would be "der Bewährte." In theory, the more consistently one can reproduce Hebrew roots with a specific family of words, the closer will one be to the original style, the more accurate will be the translation, and the more direct will be the reader's experiencing of the original text.

A third characteristic was the conscious attempt to reproduce not only the vocal effects, but the inner rhythms of the words as well. Buber and Rosenzweig, moreover, consciously used a style of German which was old, in order to give the reader the feeling of the original text. The first chapters of Genesis provide us with a good example:

Im Anfang schuf Gott den Himmel und die Erde.
Und die Erde war Wirrnis und Wüste.
Finsternis allüber Abgrund.
Braus Gottes brütend allüber den Wassern.
Da sprach Gott: Licht werde! Und Licht ward.
Dem Licht rief Gott: Tag! und der Finsternis rief er: Nacht!
Abend ward und Morgen ward: Ein Tag.

(Genesis 1.1–5)

One can sense that the style here is both dramatic and vivid, with not a superfluous word being used. The expression "Licht Werde," comes very close to the terse and abrupt Hebrew "יהי אור" while the dative effect of the Hebrew "ויקרא אלהים לאור" is caught by the German dative "Dem Licht rief Gott . . ." Even the alliterative quality of תהו ובהו is caught in "Wirrnis und Wüste." Further, Buber and Rosenzweig have consciously used an earlier style of German in order to come as close as possible to the stylistic pattern of classical Hebrew. Sensing a certain primitive and unsophisticated literary and poetic quality, they tried to recreate it by using a German that is more characteristic of an earlier period.

Again, in Genesis 2:5:

noch war alles Gestrauch des Feldes nicht auf der Erde
noch war alles Kraut des Feldes nicht geschossen
denn nicht hatte regnen lassen ER, Gott, auf die Erde,
und Mensch, Adam, war nicht, den Acker, Adama, zu bauen.

Buber and Rosenzweig convey not only the proper meaning, but they capture the distinct rhythm and emphasis of the Hebrew. The parallel structure of: וכל . . . טרם יהיה וכל . . . טרם יצמח is beautifully caught in the idiom "noch war alles . . . . nicht." Their rendering, in terms both of the rhythm of the original Hebrew and of the words which are conjoined and disjoined by trope notation is completely accurate here. The spoken, terse, rhythmic poetry is translated into German with no loss of meaning. The very use of "und Mensch, Adam, war nicht," seems so simple and direct a statement, and so true in spirit to the Hebrew which tersely says ואדם אין.

Finally, it followed that Buber and Rosenzweig wanted to come as close as they could to the original meanings of the Hebrew words, for how else could the reader perceive the intent of the author? They felt, for example, that the word שבת had to convey more than mere resting or cessation from work. They chose "feier" (to celebrate), to set it off from נוח which they render "ruhen" (resting), thus capturing something of the special spirit of Sabbath rest.

יום השבת is "Tag der Feier." "Und Gott feierte am siebenten Tag." מזבח, they argue, is more than an altar, which

KINGSLEY: *The Buber-Rosenzweig Translation of the Bible*

to them has a Christian connotation. It is a "Schlachtstaat," a place where slaughtering took place. An עֹלָה is not just a burnt offering. Since the ancient reader would have made the connection between עֹלָה and the root meaning "to go up," Buber and Rosenzweig wanted the contemporary reader to make a similar connection — hence "Hochgabe." In the Abraham story, והעלהו שם לעלה becomes "höhe ihn dort zur Hochgabe." Similarly, the קרבן is translated "Nahung" or "Darnahung," since its purpose is to bring the worshipper "near" to God (לקרב). The most unusual innovation along these lines, however, involves the translation of the Tetragrammaton. In line with his feeling that God should not be treated as a philosophical abstract, Buber argues that יהוה is the only word in the Bible for God which is a name throughout, and not a concept. שדי, אלהים, עליון etc., are all significations of some quality-power, loftiness and the like. But יהוה is pure Being — Being which makes itself known in the burning bush. The very root letters of "The Name" have a connection with the verb which means Being — הוה. And in the burning bush story, יהוה, when asked His name, replies "אהיה אשר אהיה" "I am that I am" (or, "I am Being," as some suggest). So Buber and Rosenzweig conclude that the only appropriate translation for the Tetragrammaton is the personal pronoun — ICH, DU, ER, SEIN, for in the burning bush HE reveals Himself as I. The normal translation for יהוה then, is ER (HE). "ER sprach zu Abram" is given for ויאמר יהוה אל אברהם. "ER GOTT" is given for יהוה אלהים. Only with such a translation they believed will the modern reader react in a similar way to

the way in which the ancient Hebrew reader (or hearer) reacted when he heard יהוה.

The above examples will give the reader some insight into what these two men tried to accomplish.[1]

For them, the Bible was not just an objective historical document. While they were not "orthodox" in their approach to the text, they did view it as revelation. God did speak with man, and that speech is recorded in the Bible. Somehow the translator had to make the text of the translation "speak" to the reader of today in the same way that it spoke to the generations of the past who read it and perceived it in the original.

One would like very much to be able to say that Buber and Rosenzweig succeeded in what they set out to do. Certainly, both their conception of the translator's role and their approach to Biblical style were daring and imaginative. When I first began to study their method, I was enthusiastic and even when I compared theirs with other German translations, I was moved by its poetic force and beauty. But a more intensive examination soon revealed that there were many questions to be raised, about both their entire approach to translation and its execution as well.

First, is their entire approach to Biblical style correct? Is there really a unity of language in the Bible? Is there

[1] For a fuller exposition see my thesis, "The German Translation of the Bible by Martin Buber and Franz Rosenzweig: An Analysis of Its Aim, Method, Philology and Literary Style." (Thesis done under Dr. Orlinsky for Ordination and M.A. degree, 1960; on deposit, N. Y. School of the College-Institute).

no difference between the language of Leviticus and that of Isaiah, for example, or even between that of Genesis and Leviticus? Doesn't it stand to reason, in the light of the generally accepted view that different sections of the Bible were composed at different times, that certain words, among them, "key words," perhaps might have changed in meaning or been used in different ways?

The רוח אלהים which sweeps over the waters in Genesis is obviously not the same as the רוח אלהים which fills Bezalel in Exodus, unless we reject the latest insights of scholarship. Again, even one who is sympathetic to the intentions of Buber-Rosenzweig must have moments when he wonders whether they do not overstate their case. Is not some of the so-called conscious punning and root repetition simply due to the normal style used in Biblical days, without having theological or even profound literary implications? Biblical Hebrew was, after all, a limited language in terms of vocabulary, and even in terms of the length of the alphabet, and some repetition of phrases, words and sounds was inevitable. This is not to deny that Biblical style had special and unique characteristics, but merely to warn of the dangers of finding paronomastic effects everywhere.

Even assuming Buber and Rosenzweig to be correct however, in their approach to Biblical style, it must be asked secondly whether they were able to carry their theories into the translation. Were they able, for example, to achieve "consistency" in translation? Sadly, the answer must be no. While, to mention one case in point, they would have liked to use the family of words formed from

"wahr" for the Hebrew root צדק, Buber and Rosenzweig found it impossible to do so. Thus, Noah is "ein Schuldloser," while in yet another context, צדיק is rendered "Der Gerechte." Even such words of possible theological significance as חן and חסד are translated in different ways. חן is sometimes rendered "Gunst," sometimes "Gnade," and in one instance (Gen. 6:8) "Huld." חסד is variously translated as "Güte" and "Huld."

Thirdly, and of equal importance, is a question which makes the first two questions somewhat academic. Even if we were to assume that Buber and Rosenzweig were correct in their analysis of Biblical style, and successful in translating it with the desired consistency, would the average reader of the Bible, who knows no Hebrew, and who is a product of the style and idiom of the 20th Century, be sensitive to the kind of effects Buber and Rosenzweig tried to achieve?

Subtle, paronomastic devices may have been familiar to the Biblical man, who would have expected them in his literature and who would have looked and listened for them, but they are not common to today's western reader. One suspects that many of the stylistic features which Buber and Rosenzweig describe are lost, even to the reader of the Hebrew text. How much more so would they be lost to one who reads the Bible only in translation! Should they not then have aimed for a clear, idiomatic modern translation, without worrying about and struggling with all of the stylistic subtleties, and without risking damage to both the Hebrew and German? Is it necessarily true, as Buber

KINGSLEY: *The Buber-Rosenzweig Translation of the Bible*

and Rosenzweig seem to assume *a priori*, that the closer the translation is to the original in style, the better will be the translation? To the contrary, does not such an archaic style of German, as they intentionally used in order to recreate the flavor of classical Hebrew, place a barrier between the reader and the meaning of the text?

Finally, in their zeal to come close to the original meanings of certain words, are they not prone to dreadful excesses? Is a מזבח really a slaughtering place? A check of the use of that word in the Bible would seem to show that slaughtering was usually done before the animals were placed upon the מזבח. And by what right do Buber and Rosenzweig translate יהוה with the personal pronoun? Not only do numerous practical difficulties arise which prevent them from following through all the way (בהר יהוה Auf Gottes Berg, בשם יהוה den NAMEN) but the text simply does not speak of THOU or HE or HIM. Whatever its meaning, the word is יהוה, which, far from being "ever present," came to be pronounced only on Yom Kippur by the High Priest.

A central question is raised here about their entire approach. Just how far may a translator go in trying to reproduce what he thinks the ancient man perceived when he heard or read a certain word? Such an approach leads to all manner of subjective theological intrusions which cannot be objectively defended. And perhaps this is the central fault of the Buber-Rosenzweig translation: it is essentially subjective, colored by their own theological position.

To sum up, the Buber-Rosenzweig

Bible was doomed to failure at the outset, for they tried to do the impossible. Despite Franz Rosenzweig's assertion that there is but one language for mankind, it is just not possible to say the same thing in the same way in two different languages with any degree of consistency without doing damage to one or the other. This is true under ideal conditions (one author, one language). על אחת כמה וכמה when the original itself had a development and when its creation spanned many years and involved many authors. Still, whether or not Buber and Rosenzweig were misguided in what they tried to do, and with all the faults one can find, they did at times come very close to achieving their goal. There are times when their translation comes alive, and moves one with its literary power and its loftiness.

Buber and Rosenzweig are fine poets. Not only were they masters of German, but they could sense, understand and appreciate the character of Biblical Hebrew with its inner rhythms and its unique manner of expression. At times, they were able to translate this into German. At such times, the reader is able to experience the dignity and majesty which is in the very nature of Biblical style.

Whatever one's final judgment may be, the Buber-Rosenzweig Bible is to be taken seriously. It represents a unique venture into the area of Bible translation. To be sure, it was not always successful in what it tried to accomplish, nor always acceptable in terms of scholarship. But as literature it is exciting, and as an attempt to recapture Biblical Hebrew, it is daring and imaginative.

The Stones of Nuremberg

Ralph P. Kingsley

Last summer, for the first time since I left Germany as a child of four, I returned to Nuremberg, the place of my birth. I went, not without trepidation and not because I am ready to forgive the nation which permitted there to be what Lucy Dawidowicz called "The War Against the Jews."

I went with feelings of distrust and anger, which as it turned out were not altogether unjustified. There is a renewed interest in Hitler and a resurgence of some of that old Nazi feeling not only among the old generation but among the young, who are seeing Hitler not as the vicious demonic figure he was but as a curiosity, and even as a national hero of sorts. The most recent ploy, apparently, is to remove the blame for the slaughter of Jews from Hitler and to transfer it to his supporters, Himmler, Goebbels, Goehring and company. One older man with whom we spoke said quite plainly, and with full conviction: "Hitler knew nothing. It wasn't his doing. It was the others. They knew. Not him."

I went, because whatever feelings of revulsion which I had and still have were overtaken by the desire to see my birthplace, which I left on a cold wintry night 41 years ago.

And what did I see? I saw many things. I saw the street where I was born, the house in which I lived (rebuilt after the war as was most of Nuremberg), the park in which I played, and the places where my parents had lived and worked before my birth. I saw the Jewish Community Center where the 300 Jews (mostly old) who remain in Nuremberg gather for prayer and where many of them live, for there is attached an old age home. I saw the one cousin who returned, the only relative or acquaintance left in that city which once housed our family and friends, in a Jewish community that had numbered more than 6,000. (No longer Jewish, he was raised by a Catholic family during the war, while his parents — my aunt and uncle — were in Theresienstadt.) I saw a city, prosperous and bustling, without the slightest trace of the war which had left it virtually leveled to the ground by 1945.

But mainly I saw stones — stones which had their own message and story which they told with eloquent silence.

The history of the Jewish People is contained in stone. Anyone who has ever set foot in Israel will attest to that. The history of Jewish heroism is found in the ruins of Masada where a small group of zealots held back an entire Roman army for two years until they could hold out no longer and died a martyrs' death.

The story of Jewish suffering is built into the outer walls of Jerusalem, torn down and rebuilt with new layers heaped upon old as each era of oppression commenced anew.

The story of the Holocaust is set into the ground at Yad Vashem, engraved in simple black stones which contain such names as Auschwitz, Dachau, Birchenau and Treblinka.

And the story of Jewish survival is etched into the white stones in the military cemetery, arranged by wars—beginning in the days of the British Mandate, and continuing through 1948, 1956, 1970, 1973, and most recently, 1976—where Yonathan Natanyahu, who was killed in Entebbe, lies buried in a modest grave.

The stones I saw in Germany were perhaps less dramatic. But they too revealed much—not only in what they said, but in what, at times, they did not say.

On the way to Nuremberg, we stopped in Munich, a city of over a million, remembered for its beer halls and the infamous Munich Pact of 1939 which dismembered Czechoslovakia, and caused Neville Chamberlain to promise "peace in our time." There, on the site where once the great Synagogue stood, was a stone monument. It said: "*Zachor*—Remember! Here stood the great Synagogue of Munich from 1887 to June 11, 1938 when it was destroyed." Seemingly as an afterthought, there follows the sentence: "On Nov. 20, 1938, synagogues were destroyed throughout

Impressive, at first glance. Until one begins to ask oneself what meaning those few words have to the German child growing up. What can he know about Hitler and the horror of Kristallnacht from that dispassionate statement? How can he begin to feel some sense of the nightmare of those days from that sterile description? The slaughter of six million, the utter contempt for human life and its dignity and worth.

The stone tells a story to those of us who know—in what it says but even more in what it does not say.

In Nuremberg, too, there was a stone of the "here stood" variety, although much smaller. Moreover, this was far less visible than the one in Munich. It was surrounded by pretty plantings which had grown over it. I would not have seen it had not my cousin's wife pointed it out to us. How ironic! A reminder of the grimmest, blackest period in the history of humankind, covered over by pretty green things that made it seem as if nothing had ever happened.

To add to the irony, on that same day, Chancellor Schmidt was quoted in the German papers as saying one couldn't apply moral principles to international affairs, in the manner President Carter sought to do. I wondered whether he had ever seen the stone?

But the most revealing stones were the ones in the cemetery where my grandfather and great uncles and distant cousins are buried. The cemetery was so peaceful, so pretty, filled not only with stones reset and re-engraved by loving relatives and loyal friends who survived, after having been desecrated into a shambles during the Hitler days, but filled with trees which provided shade and beauty. I thought of Gray's famous "Elegy in a Country Churchyard:

Beneath those rugged elms, that yew-
    trees
shade where heaves the turf in many a
    mouldering heap
Each in his narrow cell forever laid
The rude forefathers of the hamlet
    sleep.

As I looked more closely, I was suddenly struck by a peculiar phenomenon. The dates on these stones stop in 1938.

Oh, there were two or three dated as late as 1940, 41 or 42, and there were a handful from after 1946. But only a handful. It was as if an entire generation of people suddenly disappeared.

In point of fact, they did. The ones who lay buried here were perhaps the fortunate ones, whose lives came to an end before the end came for the life of German Jewry. They were spared the torture, the agony, the degradation and the death that awaited those who, like my paternal grandmother, were sent away to the camps, never to return.

As I stood at those quiet graves, it struck me, as never before: Who will take the place of that missing generation? Who will transmit Torah to their unborn children, and to the unborn children and grandchildren of the rest of the six million who perished in that Holocaust? But that is silly. If they perished, there are no children or grandchildren.

But then, who will remain to care for the stones upon which their story is written?

I stood with my two sons and said Kaddish. As we intoned the ancient words, I realized more than ever how critical it is to raise and educate Jewish children, especially against the gloomy predictions of some demographers who warn us of the dire consequences of a diminishing Jewish birth rate, whether through the conscious refusal to have children or through intermarriage. By way of example, I thought of the Carter Administration's three "Jewish" cabinet members, Messrs. Brown, Blumenthal and Schlesinger—and how six Jewish grandparents have 13 non-Jewish grandchildren. Is that what the future holds? And I remembered Elie Wiesel's interpretation of the Akeda story as being the first Holocaust, with Isaac as the first survivor. "The end of Isaac would con-

note the end of a prodigious adventure . . . One cannot conceive of a more crushing or more devastating anguish [than to] have lived and suffered and caused others to suffer for nothing."

Then, back to the stones. Who will remain to care for them? The answer is obvious. We survivors, who are Isaac, must live, not only so that the "others" will not have suffered for nothing, but so that we can care for the stones. There is no one else.

RABBI KINGLEY, *spiritual leader of Temple Sinai of North Dade, is president of AJCongress' Florida Southeast Region.*

NOVEMBER 1978

My Teacher, Dr. Samuel Atlas— A Reminiscence

Ralph P. Kingsley

It is more than a year since a brief announcement appeared in the newspapers stating that Professor Samuel Atlas of the Hebrew Union College-Jewish Institute of Religion had died. To most, the announcement would have meant little. He was a Jewish scholar who never went "popular," so to speak. He was known to other scholars, and by the students he taught—most of them Reform rabbis. I was one of those students. He was a man whom I adored and whose death deeply touched me, not only because it came so suddenly and, as always, too soon, but because he was one of the major influences on my rabbinic thinking.

His physical appearance is as vivid in my mind today as it was when I was ordained eighteen years ago. He was a little man, baldish and pudgy, with a round face and jowls that vibrated whenever he would shake his head, somewhat in the manner of the late actor Zadie Sackell. Having been born in Lithuania, he had a thick Yiddish accent which he never lost, despite his total command of English. But though he was small physically, his mind and his wealth of learning was of extraordinary vastness—so much so that some of his students dubbed him "Charlie" Atlas, after the strong man and body builder of popular fame.

He came from a rationalist rabbinic background and pursued essentially two areas, Talmud and philosophy. Both befitted his Litvak origin, and he brought both to life in the classroom. His philosophical knowledge ranged from the classics to the medieval to the modern period. He was as much at home with Plato, Kant, and Schopenhauer as he was with Jehudah Ha-Levi, Maimonides, and—*lehavdil*—Martin Buber, whom he thought shallow.

Dr. Atlas could swim through the "sea of Talmud" at any depth

---

RALPH P. KINGSLEY is rabbi of Temple Sinai of North Dade, North Miami Beach, Florida.

Fall, 1979

RALPH P. KINGSLEY

and never miss a stroke. Not only did he have surface knowledge of that immense work in its entirety, but he was able to dive far beneath the surface into the depths as only a man who was a philosopher as well as a legalist could.

He was impatient with stupidity, and even more impatient with arrogance. He never did come to terms with the American style that permits a student—no matter how low his level of learning—to interrupt and challenge the professor. He did not believe in the equality of all who happened to be studying together. Rather, the most learned was the one whose opinion was to be the most highly regarded and accepted. He used to rail against the egalitarianism of the American classroom that permitted an atmosphere in which everyone's answer was as good as everyone else's. "How can it be?," he used to ask. "This one is right, and this one is right, and this one is right. It can't be so." And he would shake his head until redness flushed his cheeks. For him, there was only *one* right at any given time. In his classroom, he was it. We students were not his equals, not there to tell him he was wrong. We were there to learn. Needless to say, he also had no use of any relativistic system that could allow for more than *one* right and *one* wrong at any given moment.

I often thought of Dr. Atlas in my early days in the rabbinate, when I had to listen to laymen who knew very little tell me what Reform Judaism was and was not. The implication was that they knew it better than I, or at least as well as I. After all, in a society where all are equal, everyone has a right to his opinion—even if based on ignorance. I still think of him when I see and hear the atmosphere of "anything goes" in which we live, the atmosphere that judges everything by "relative" standards and hesitates to call anything wrong.

It was *the search for moral truth* that was Dr. Atlas' greatest interest. Whatever he taught us, that was the hidden agenda. For him, the Torah and the Talmud were nothing less than exemplifications of that search *through law*. Jewish law was no whimsical set of rules. Its uniqueness lay in its attempt to create that which was most true and most right and, thus, most beneficial for our world. He taught law—in our case Jewish law—as only a moral philosopher could. That was the singularity of his approach.

If Hillel instituted a *prosbul*—a legal fiction that countermanded the Torah law of the sabbatical year—it was for the sake of a higher ethical purpose, namely, to protect the lender and the borrower, both of whom had become disadvantaged prior to the sabbatical year. If

MY TEACHER, DR. SAMUEL ATLAS—A REMINISCENCE

there was the creation of a divorce decree called a *get* of which the Bible has no mention, it was to protect the woman and to grant her certain rights. There was no section of law, or of philosophy for that matter, from which Professor Atlas did not derive some ethical principle.

I left his class believing—and I still do—that a law which is not *ethical* is not *just*. Germany had laws between 1933 and 1945. But they were *unethical* laws. A nation whose laws are not founded on ethics must ultimately destroy itself.

Dr. Atlas taught me another truth. He taught me that the unseeable is at times more powerful than all else. An *idea* can, after all, shape reality and effect change. Reality is simply the world as it is, not as it could be. He called himself a "critical idealist." The idea as it takes form in the human mind has the power to mold the universe. For example, there is no such thing as a perfect triangle in the real world; it exists only in the mind of man. Yet mathematics would not be possible without it. Such is the power of an idea.

Would there have been an Israel if Theodor Herzl had not dreamed a dream long before it became reality?

Even absolute justice is an ideal. Dr. Atlas taught us that "an eye for an eye" is ideal law, but impossible to achieve in reality. The eye of a proofreader does not have the same worth to him as that of a streetcleaner. Nor does the hand of a surgeon have the same importance to him as the hand of a general practitioner, who might be able to get along with one hand. Yet the aim of justice is to achieve an absolute equality; the ideal goal is to reward and punish in a manner that provides equal recompense for what has been done right or wrong. The task of the real world is mostly closely to approximate that ideal end.

Professor Atlas always wore a *kippah* when he taught us Talmud or when he came with us to our weekly chapel service on Friday morning. Yet he was a Reform Jew in the most classical sense. He saw Judaism as a rational, ethical system—not perfect but moving toward perfection.

Most of all, he understood that a system which becomes rigid—whether from an orthodoxy on the right or on the left (e.g., some fixated expressions of Reform Judaism)—fails to come to terms with Judaism's inner dynamic, which is change and adaptability. The development of Jewish law was, for him, ample evidence of that truth. For Dr. Atlas the very labels Reform, Conservative and Orthodox (and he could be critical of all three, as well as of Reconstructionism) were inadequate. "There are only two kinds of Judaism,"

Fall, 1979

215

RALPH P. KINGSLEY

he would say; "dogmatic Judaism and philosophical Judaism." His meaning was plain. He had no use for dogmatists on the right or left. A reasoned, open, philosophical approach might not lead to uniformity of practice, but it could provide a common universe of discourse and serve as a unifying factor.

I was not one of those who wrote his rabbinic thesis under Dr. Atlas, but of all my teachers—and each of them influenced me in some way—I believe that Dr. Atlas gave me perhaps the most practical and lasting tools with which to shape my rabbinate: a respect for reason, not as end but as a means; an appreciation for the ethical undergirdings of Jewish Law; an aversion to dogmatism; and, above all, a deep commitment to the power of the idea and the ideal. If some of those thoughts emerge in my teaching and my sermons from time to time, then it is Dr. Atlas who must be given the credit. And if I am at all typical, I suspect that Professor Atlas' thinking will be among us for a long time to come, even though his earthly presence is gone.

But then, as he would say; "How could it be otherwise? It must be so!" For ideas have a life of their own that transcend the boundaries of human mortality.

Observations

Singing the Jewish Blues
And Other Paeans to Assimilation

Ralph P. Kingsley

The "Jazz Singer" was a hit with the young. They loved the music. The romance and the triumph of the American Spirit—the victory of youth and individualism over age and tradition—spoke to them.

The elderly loved it too for it evoked memories of earlier versions—perhaps even the 1927 original starring Al Jolson. It made them feel young again.

Only I didn't love it. The film, which tells the story of a young man (Neil Diamond) who comes from a long line of cantors and his desire to become a jazz singer, is simplistic and misleading. The plot lacks verisimilitude thus calling its entire premise into question. The message, moreover, which the movie sends about intermarriage and assimilation—especially to young Jews—is distorted and damaging to the cause of Jewish life.

First, the movie pretends that it is based on reality. But are we really to infer that a Lower East Side Synagogue would have an active congregation and a flourishing Hebrew School in 1980? Most Lower East Side Synagogues, once centers of activity, are now boarded up and opened only for an occasional minyan, or more likely, a tour group.

Second, casting Neil Diamond as a cantor is akin to having Frank Sinatra portray Luciano Pavorotti. Perry Como's *Kol Nidre* is more authentic than Diamond's. It isn't that I don't like Neil Diamond. To the contrary. I just wouldn't choose him to be my cantor. At least Al Jolson, the star of the original "Jazz Singer" had sung in Jewish choirs and was born to a cantorial family.

Third, the image of the cantor speeding through *Adon Olam* so that he could rush to the recording studio to cut a record—on *Yom Tov*—is in the worst of taste and degrading to the cantorate.

Nonetheless, the latest "Jazz Singer" like its predecessors, does deal with problems which serious Jews confront daily and which have bearing on Jewish survival.

We Jews live in two worlds. Shabbat, *Yom Tov* and concern for Jewish survival conflict at times with our secular society which reserves Friday night for socials and Saturday for shopping and going to the beauty parlor. We want our kids to love being Jewish, but we also want them to have dance or music or drama lessons, all of which seem to take place on Saturday morning. We want them not to be different. So what shall it be? Teams or Torah? Athletics or praying?

Such dilemmas are minor in themselves but they are symbolic of greater problems, not the least of them—intermarriage.

Americans are love-oriented. We are conditioned to believe that love conquers all—including tensions which may arise because of our racial, religious, social, economic or cultural backgrounds. Living in a free and open society, with emotions unbridled, means that intermarriage will be inevitable. But intermarriage is also inevitably detrimental to the Jewish people. It takes no great insight to understand that when a Jew "marries out" the chances of his rearing Jewish children are lessened.

Thus, the *coup de grâce* of the "Jazz Singer" is the way the film caricatures Diamond's two wives. The first wife, Jewish and pious, is sweet, innocent and dull, wanting nothing more than to be an obedient child-bearing companion. The second wife, not Jewish, is understanding, highly-principled, concerned, "alive" and fulfilling.

In spite of itself, this movie must make us consider how we can bridge the two worlds in which we live and whether or not we can only participate in one *or* another. Can we on the one hand be strict and disciplined in our Jewish loyalty, and on the other hand, be freely and openly a part of the western society in which we live?

I think of two responses. The first concerns the debate Shalom Aleichem's Tevye the milkman has in "Fiddler on the Roof." Tevya, that brilliant example of the Jew caught in a world of changing values, discovers that his daughter is about to marry a non-Jew. Back and forth he argues with himself: "On the one hand she's my daughter. On the other hand, will she give me Jewish grandchildren? On the one hand, I love her. On the other, she is not considering my feelings and her family." And so on and on--on the one hand and on the other, until, finally he says: "On the other hand . . . there is no other hand."

I think too of that brilliant rabbi and writer, the late Milton Steinberg, who was a product of the secular world. Yet he found his roots in his Jewish heritage and understood their profound importance.

In his novel *As A Driven Leaf*, Steinberg writes about the fictionalized life of Elisha Ben Abuyah, a rabbi who leaves the seemingly retrictive world of Judaism for the freedom of pagan Rome, foresaking the one for the other.

Elisha insightfully says: "A man has happiness if he possesses three things— those whom he loves and who love him in turn; confidence in the world and continued existence of the group of which he is a part; and last of all, a truth by which he may order his being."

Each of us pursues love and truth. What we sometimes overlook or do not fully comprehend is that they are nothing without a relationship to the group of which we are a part. The problem with the "Jazz Singer" is its suggestion that we need to escape from our group in order to find happiness. But that suggestion denies the deeper truth of who we really are, and what type of obligation that identity entails.

The "Jazz Singer" and other works of that ilk will continue to plague us, claiming to represent a "higher" truth and reality than that which some of us are ready to accept. The task for those who care about Jewish life and Jewish survival is to create a sufficiently "creative" environment within Jewish life that will make the seductive lure of the "other world" less attractive. ☐

RABBI RALPH P. KINGSLEY, *president, AJCongress' Southeast Region and a national vice president of the executive committee, is rabbi of Temple Sinai of North Dade, Florida.*

JUNE 1981

How Henry Kissinger Became My Cousin

RALPH P. KINGSLEY

Henry Kissinger, former Secretary of State and National Security Advisor, is a distant relative of mine, a fact that is probably of considerably more interest to me than it is to him. I know that because I received no answer when I first wrote to wish him well on his appointment to high office in the Nixon administration. It took the intervention of my congressman's secretary with Kissinger's secretary to get me a curt reply acknowledging my congratulatory note. That was when I first discovered the real power in this country to be in the hands of secretaries.

Notwithstanding the rebuff (I have been rejected before) I feel a strange sense of pride in my "Kissinger Connection." It comes from the *yiches* of the implied "international connection." It comes also from the remarkable history of the Jewish people, about whose existence I never cease to wonder. Here we are, scattered throughout the world, battered by a Holocaust which destroyed one third of our population, and besieged by the pressures of intermarriage and assimilation, not to speak of continuing attacks upon us by hostile nations. Yet, we are still here — after all these centuries.

Part of the "miracle of Jewish survival" became obvious when I discovered my family history. I have a cousin in Herzliah named Martin Kissinger — a second cousin of my father's to be exact — who undertook to trace the Kissinger family tree some years ago. The result was an initial narrative history, written in German, which came into my hands in 1974. It was constructed from the memories of various family members who live in far-flung places, and from records in the archives of Roedelsee and Bad Kissingen, as well as records in the Catholic diocese in Roedelsee in the southern part of Germany. The Germans, with their penchant for organization, left accurate records going back hundreds of years.

More recently, my cousin Martin perfected that family history, updated it, and had it diagrammed so that one could quickly see who was related to whom and how. It traces the Kissinger family tree to a certain Meyer ben Loeb, who lived from 1767 to 1838, and who took the name Kissinger in 1817 — probably from the area he left to come to Roedelsee, namely, Bad Kissingen. Before then, he had grown up in a place called Klein-Eibstadt. He was apparently a teacher by profession, although in the records

Ralph P. Kingsley is the rabbi of Temple Sinai of North Dade, North Miami Beach, Florida.

MY SPIRITUAL JOURNEY

of the Catholic diocese his occupation is listed also as butcher. My cousin speculates that he may have been a *mohel* (which is not to imply that *mohelim* are butchers — heaven forbid).

It is from Meyer ben Loeb that the Kissinger family originates. It does so in two branches, for Meyer married twice and sired two separate families. From his first wife, Marianne, who died in childbirth in 1812, came two sons. The one, Loeb, became the ancestor of my side of the family. His second wife, Schoenlein, bore four daughters and six sons, only one of whom seems to have had a large family. From that prolific son, Abraham Kissinger, comes the other line, to which Henry belongs. Thus, Meyer ben Loeb was the great-great-grandfather, four generations back, of both my father, Albert, and of "cousin" Henry, although in each case the great-great-grandmother was different. Alas, my family and Henry's come from separate branches of the Kissinger family tree. Generationally, Henry and my father are third cousins, but in truth, I suppose they are only half-cousins. And that is how Henry Kissinger became my cousin, or to be precise, third half-cousin once removed.

What was more exciting and significant than discovering the nature of our "relationship," however, was the discovery that I come from a family of teachers, although I must admit that most of them come from the "other branch." The discovery of so many teachers in our past somehow gives much more authority to my choice of the rabbinate as a career.

As I studied my genealogy, I began to have a remarkable feeling of family tradition, as transmitted from generation to generation. Our traceable history goes back only two hundred years, out of a four-thousand-year Jewish history — the tip of an iceberg. Yet even those few years give one a marvelous sense of the loyalty that has made for Jewish survival.

Meyer ben Loeb was born in an era when Jews first were beginning to gain some entrée into the Western world. Remember that Moses Mendelssohn, the so-called father of modern Judaism, who taught that a person could be a Jew and a Western person at the same time, lived in the latter part of the eighteenth century.

Yet, despite the seductive appeal of Western civilization, my relatives of earlier generations *did not* defect en masse, the fact that it would probably have been easier to live as non-Jews notwithstanding.

It was not until my generation that there were some seeming defections. One cousin, who was hidden with Catholics during World War II by his parents, no longer practices Judaism. Another is married to a non-Jewish girl and I do not know how he will raise his daughter. Nor dare I predict what will be in the next generation.

But so far, the family has remained remarkably Jewish. Even cousin Henry, despite his second marriage to Nancy McGuiness, has two children by his first marriage who are being Jewishly reared by their mother, also remarried, albeit Jewishly. His father, Louis, is, of course, quite Orthodox.

HOW HENRY KISSINGER BECAME MY COUSIN

What has made for that loyalty, I'm not sure. That it is there, however, is dramatically evidenced in my family tree. One sees it in the transmission of first names, some of them out-and-out German, but many of them obviously Jewish. At the very time when the ghettos were opening, Meyer ben Loeb, who was not only prolific but pious, was naming his children Isaac, Nathan, Abraham, Esther, Salomon, and David, names which still recur in later generations.

Last names, of course, do change, both through the marriage of the daughters and through conscious acts. Our name became Kingsley in 1940, two years after we came to America, at a time when German-sounding names were not popular here. So my father and my uncle "anglicized," using a name suggested by a cousin who had come to America from Germany via England, where he stayed with someone named Kingsley.

Somehow I have always felt bad about that even though I had nothing to do with it. Knowing that third cousins in Israel also changed their names has not lessened the discomfort. Their desire was undoubtedly also to make a "new start" and to move beyond their Germanic ancestry by Hebraizing their name. They simply took the first, middle, and last letters of Kissinger and made Keynar, probably related to *kinor,* or "violin." While I am not happy about the result, I accept the reality, knowing that the practice is a common and legitimate one, both here and in Israel. In any case, it is too complicated to change back, and then too, "what's in a name?" The roots are well sunk, and the tree which Hitler sought to cut down has given birth to new saplings — appropriately in the two centers of Jewish life.

Not all of the Kissingers were as fortunate as my family here or that of our Israeli cousins, however. The family tree conveys that message too. In microcosm it shows the enormity of the effect of the Holocaust on our people. The diagrammed portion alone does not, perhaps, sufficiently tell the story. While it clearly shows the dead ends, of which, alas, there are all too many, it doesn't give the reasons for them. To be sure, it doesn't take great intellect to figure out that some of those dead ends resulted from offspring not marrying, others from the fact that no children were born, and still others from premature death. But when one reads the narrative together with the genealogical tables, one discovers another dimension with which all Jews of our time live — the stunning effect of the Holocaust on our generations.

Firsthand, I knew only of a single grandmother who was sent away in 1942. Fortunately, the rest of my immediate family had the foresight and means to leave in time.

But I discovered so many who did not leave — who perished; mothers and daughters, fathers and sons. Here was Joseph, a grandson of Meyer's, a teacher, four of whose five children were killed by the Nazis. Here was Jette, a granddaughter, three of whose five were killed. Here were great-grandchildren Ferdinand and Julius, again teachers, who perished.

Multiply those statistics by other families. Reflect on how many stumps of trees remain which will never be sources of new seedlings. Reflect on all of the children who will never be born and whose names will never appear on a genealogical table.

Yet we did survive. And here is one more interesting aspect of the genealogy. Many settled in *Israel*, and live there today, as indicated above, rearing their children in that free and Jewish environment. What would we have done or do without Israel? Other considerations aside, a look at the narrative of the genealogy gives dramatic evidence of how important that land was and is to our people and its life. Here strangely, it is my side of the family, from Meyer's first marriage, that has produced the Zionists. One of my father's brothers settled in Palestine, in fact, and died there before Israel was reborn a state.

Not that I don't have relatives all over the rest of the world too, I discovered, from South America to South Africa, to Switzerland, to Sweden, Portugal, and all the way south to Australia. If ever you had doubts about whether or not we Jews are an international people, just look at your own genealogy and I'm sure the doubts will vanish. The term "wandering Jew" is not the product of an idle imagination. It is based on solid reality caused by the fact that we have time and again been driven out of places that we thought were hospitable to us and forced to seek places of refuge — and to those places, especially the United States of America, we are profoundly grateful.

But when the moment of truth comes, it is only Israel that is truly our own. We've done well elsewhere. But I wonder if there is any place in the world that offers quite the sense of inner security that comes from knowing you are with your own. And somehow, there must be a meaning in the fact that of all the Kissingers, it is one who lives in Israel, where ultimately we find our original roots, who took the initiative to trace our modern roots.

To end where I began: The great miracle is that we are here; that we can talk about our lineage, our origins, our roots; that we can *qvell* over the fact that we have an unbroken history as a people that binds us together, regardless of where we may be living at any moment in time.

The reason for this is precisely that we have always been motivated by two foci. We have had a sense of *history;* a sense that our past has meaning and is worthy of our efforts to learn it and to perpetuate it.

But the other reason is that we have also had a sense of destiny; of a future that was special; of a role that was unique; of a task that needed fulfilling — to make the world better.

It is undoubtedly the greatness of our yesterdays that poses both the challenge and the possibility of an even greater tomorrow.

In Search of a Place to Pray

Ralph P. Kingsley

One of the things to which I looked forward with great anticipation as the day of my retirement drew near was *shul*-hopping. Yes, I admit that I am addicted to Sabbath and holiday worship. I am one of those rare Reform Jews who always goes to synagogue on Shabbat and on *Yom Tov*, whether I am at home or away on a trip. Not only do I believe it is what a Jew ought to do on our days of celebration, but I actually enjoy going. The only time I have missed doing so over the years is when I have been sick or in a place where there was no synagogue, in which case I davened at home.

So when I became rabbi emeritus of the synagogue I had served for thirty-one years, and wanting to stay out of the way of my successor, I began to go to Sabbath services (evening and morning) in a variety of area congregations—Reform, Conservative, Orthodox, Sephardic, and Ashkenazic. In the more traditional synagogues (less so in the Reform), I would frequently be given an *aliyah*. Oftentimes, it was because the rabbi or someone from the congregation recognized me, but even where I was noticed as a new face, I was extended that courtesy. We Reform Jews could learn a lesson from that. For a while, I was particularly attracted to a certain Sephardic synagogue, not only because of the different nature of its *minhag* and their *nusah* but because they did not repeat the *Musaf Tefilah*, thus completing the service by 11:45 A.M. That was fine, until one week a *Bar Mitzvah* and two *ufrufen* were added to the service, and with that came an endless string of *aliyot*, thus lengthening the service by more than half an hour. That does not even begin to account for the boredom factor in having to listen to the same section of the Torah chanted again and again and again. I have been afraid to go back there ever since.

Of late, I find myself going, most often, to an Orthodox *minyan* nearby that meets in a little house that has been transformed into a *shul*. There is no rabbi and no cantor and no Torah explanation or

RALPH P. KINGSLEY (NY60) is rabbi emeritus of Temple Sinai, North Miami Dade, Florida.

drash, except on those rare occasions when there is a special guest who may be asked to speak. The service is essentially lay-driven by a group of knowledgeable and committed Jews, many of them Holocaust survivors who range in age from their eighties down. All of them, except me, live close enough to walk to *shul*. Although I would prefer to walk as well—not so much because of the constraints of *halakhah* but because it would make the day more special—I drive because to walk three miles in either direction in the south Florida heat would not enhance the joy of the Sabbath. They seem to understand this. So far, no one has complained, although I must admit to feeling a bit awkward about the whole thing. They use the Art Scroll *siddur* and the Art Scroll *humash*, and the service is entirely in Hebrew. In season, when attendance is maximal, there are perhaps sixty men there on Saturday morning (fewer on Friday night) and a third as many women, none of whom seems to mind sitting behind the *mehitzah*.

So why do I, a Reform Jew from birth, enjoy praying in an environment that I did not grow up with, and that lacks many of the elements that I sought to bring into the service that I tried to create in my active rabbinic years: intelligibility, a level of musical and aesthetic richness, contemporary relevance, intellectual coherence, equality of the sexes, and beyond which is, in many ways, very much at odds with my personal theology?

The answer has to do, not so much, with the words that, in Jewish-style, I can interpret to suit my own belief system. Rather, it is the fact that the people who gather to pray in that little do-it-yourself *minyan* are there for only three reasons: they *want* to be; it is Shabbat (or *Yom Tov*) and that is where a Jew *ought* to be; and they understand that regular worship is a *mitzvah* that a Jew is duty bound to fulfill. There are no recalcitrant children whose parents have dropped them at the door. There is not the Bar Mitzvah crowd that cannot wait for the service to end so that they can party. There is no attempt to pander to the lowest common denominator in order to make the experience meaningful. There only are Jews who have gathered to pray and who take seriously all that that implies, Jews who respect the tradition of prayer and the structure of the service. They know the Jewish calendar and understand the additions that are called for on special Sabbaths. They are aware that by coming to synagogue, a Jew will not only always have a sense of who he or she is but of where he or she is in the grand scheme of Jewish life. *Shabbat Parah*, for example, alerts us to the coming of springtime.

RALPH P. KINGSLEY

We feel the winds of freedom blowing and start to think about ridding our homes of *hametz*. *Rosh Ḥodesh Elul* directs our thoughts to prayers of forgiveness and to an awareness of the fast-approaching turn of the year, an especially awesome period for the pulpit rabbi. It is not as if I did not know these things before, but experiencing them in that very humble setting helps raise my own level of awareness. What goes on in the service is, after all, a reflection of Jewish time and Jewish values.

On a more practical level, the morning service begins at 9 A.M. and always is over well before noon, in time for me to get home for a leisurely *Shabbat* lunch with my wife and, if I am lucky, with a grandchild or two. On Friday night, prayers begin and end in time to get me home for a Shabbat dinner with family and friends, which I missed out on during all those years of officiating at late *Shabbat* services.

By way of contrast, I have had a very difficult time finding that kind of environment in a Reform service. Rather, I have seen some very strange things when I have attended a variety of Reform synagogues at home and away. In one instance, I called for the time of a *Yom Tov* service and was told by the rabbi: "By the way, you should know that we won't be reading the Torah. The worship committee has agreed that we read it only when the *Yom Tov* falls on a Saturday, Monday, or Thursday." In another synagogue, I went to a Saturday-morning service but found, much to my chagrin, that there was no Torah service, despite a *minyan*. The reason? Since there was Torah discussion, it was not necessary to take out the scroll. In yet another location, the congregation observed the second day of *Rosh Hashanah* but omitted the sounding of the *shofar* as a compromise in order to shorten the service.

I have encountered the reading of the wrong *haftarot*, on those mornings when I had looked forward to the special reference to *Rosh Ḥodesh* or the onset of the month of *Nisan*. Apart from the annoyance of an expectation unfulfilled, there is the teacher in me feeling sad about a learning opportunity missed. Is it not knowing or just an attitude of not caring because, in Reform Judaism, each individual is free to do whatever finds favor in his or her eyes? Neither speaks well for us. Nor does it speak well when the service itself is arranged in such a way that its carefully fashioned structure is distorted. In the interest of time, I have seen colleagues skip the *Modim*, the very prayer that tradition teaches will still need to be said even after the Messiah comes. I was at a *Sukkot*-evening service expecting the appropriate holiday additions and melodies, only to be treated, instead, to a regular Shabbat-eve service read by the evening's Bat Mitzvah. I suspect this omission was because someone had not checked the calendar in advance and, once programmed, it seemed risky to ask the Bat Mitzvah to change course. In another instance, again an evening Bat Mitzvah, the service jumped from *Mi Khamokha* to the Torah service, with omission of the *Tefilah*. If time were a problem, why not have asked worshippers at least to pray that portion in silence? It would have saved time and still have been authentic. As is, the message to the Bat Mitzvah and to the rest of us was "anything goes." But, probably worse, no one even noticed or cared.

Having "been there," I think I understand the ongoing struggle to get our Reform Jews into the synagogue, on both Friday night and Saturday morning, as well as on *Yom Tov*. We have become accustomed to dealing with a population that is often uninterested and uncaring when it comes to prayer, the new interest in "spirituality" and even the creation of a new prayerbook notwithstanding. Our responses are many and varied, ranging from scholar weekends and guest speakers to lay participation in prayers, to the scheduling of alternative services—an earlier Kabbalat Shabbat in place of or in addition to the more customary late service, and/or alternative services on Saturday morning for those who want to avoid the Bar Mitzvah crowd or who just desire a less formal environment. (This is not to say, incidentally, that a Sabbath morning service need be an unspiritual experience because of the presence of a Bar or Bat Mitzvah. I have been to synagogues where the focus remains on Shabbat and Torah and not on the Bar or Bat Mitzvah; where the Bar or Bat Mitzvah is an adjunct to the service and not the reverse; where the rabbi has taught Torah in a most engaging way, despite the presence of many strangers.) I have no doubt that our colleagues, in their own ways, are trying hard to be responsive to new needs and circumstances in the ever-changing landscape of Reform Judaism, despite an environment that frequently pits the rabbi who wants more against congregants who want less. But with it all, to this interested observer, something has gone amiss.

I do not lay blame entirely on the rabbi. Rather, I believe it is the very culture of Reform that causes colleagues who have created wonderful congregations and whose friendship I cherish, to do things that I consider strange, at best, and destructive, at worst. Yet, it is precisely that culture that is keeping me from worshipping

RALPH P. KINGSLEY

regularly at a Reform congregation. I am never quite sure what I will encounter. To be sure, I would like to be moved; I would like to be uplifted. But most of all, I would like to have an authentic Jewish experience. Am I not entitled to that? Is not any Jew who comes into one of our synagogues?

Granted, over the years I have become something of a liturgical purist and so I may be a bit more sensitive and critical than the average person. But are there not norms that one has a right to expect when one goes into a synagogue, whatever its affiliation? And do we Reform rabbis, as representatives and teachers of a rich and historic heritage, not have an obligation to make sure that those norms are followed so that people who come into our synagogues to pray can feel totally at home irrespective of which stream of Judaism they choose to swim in?

We live at a time when more of our young families are deepening their Jewish commitments. Reform is no longer the refuge of the assimilationists. There are those in our midst who want to become serious Jews. I believe that they would like to do so in the context of Reform. We owe them more than we are giving them. If we short change them, they will go elsewhere as I find myself doing.

WA